HIGHEST QUALITY

Tina Turner recalls the two times her longtime beau, Erwin Bach, asked her to marry him. After three years of dating in 1989, he proposed; twenty-three years later, on a voyage around the Mediterranean, she said yes. Tina discusses how her feelings on marriage have changed over time. Erwin proposed to Tina because he felt she deserved a serious relationship when she turned fifty. Tina felt uncertain about marriage despite her strong feelings for him. She is realistic about the challenges that come with marriage since she has had mixed results in the past. Tina like the dynamic that they had and their connection, so she was hesitant to change anything about it. The next time Erwin proposed was on their trip in the Mediterranean. Tina remembers the perfect backdrop and how Herbert had asked their mutual friend Sergio for help in creating an amazing romantic experience. The excitement mounts as they set sail for Scorpios, the Greek island made renowned as the former getaway of Onassis. Tina describes the day they spent on the boat with their friends, taking in the sights and relaxing. Tina senses a change in the mood as the evening unfolds, one of expectation and excitement. The all-white-clad visitors turn their focus to Er Win, who kneels down in front of Tina holding a little package. He makes his second marriage proposal to her in flawless English. Tina's pals are overtaken with emotion; some cry, while others express their elation aloud. At the ripe old age of seventy-three, Tina enthusiastically accepts Erwin's proposal, accepting love and commitment that had previously been difficult for her. The conversation then turns to Tina's prior marriage to Ike Turner, which she compares with her upcoming nuptials. She talks of growing up in Nut bush, a small town in the South where big weddings were unusual. By the moment she was born, both sets of parents were married, or none of them had married at all. Tina thinks back on her marriage to Ike and how it wasn't a "real wedding," explaining why she doesn't have any wedding day illusions. Tina Turner's autobiography delves into her conflicted thoughts about marriage and her maturation as a person. She struggles with commitment and change, worried about how it could affect her relationship with Erwin. Tina initially hesitated to accept Erwin's marriage proposal, but she finally felt ready to say "yes" after being in a beautiful environment with her loved ones. Tina Turner discusses the events leading up to her wedding to Ike Turner. She elaborates on Ike's proposition, which she says was motivated only by money. Tina was hesitant to marry Ike at first, but after considering their shared work and four children, she ultimately decided to give in. Tina remembers Ike's proposal to her and says he didn't do anything particularly romantic. Ike, who had been wedded many times and was involved in several relationships, thought that marrying Tina would help him resolve a financial dispute with one of his ex-wives. Tina stresses the difficulty they had in adjusting to life as a mixed family with four children. Tina wanted to put out an appearance of propriety for the wedding. She put on her nicest outfit, complete with a brown hat with a broad brown brim. Tina says that she wanted to seem more wedding-appropriate than her normal stage seductive self. She lacked instruction in social affairs, so she developed her own unique sense of style via trial and error, observation of the people she met, and the pages of fashion magazines. Tina and Ike's driver Duke was a family friend, so the two of them got in the vehicle together on their wedding day. Ike, ever the opportunist, felt that Tijuana, Mexico, was going to be the ideal location for a hastily organized wedding. Tina recalls how nasty and honky-tonk it was in Tijuana back then. Tina and the groom discovered a dingy little office where the final wedding paperwork had been finished. Not even the standard wedding fare of kisses, toasts, and congratulations was there. The event failed to inspire any optimism about the years to come. But what happened after the wedding was much more upsetting for Tina. Ike insisted on having his way, so on the night of their marriage the couple visited a whorehouse. Tina says she's ashamed to tell her tale for the first time. Tina Turner opens out about how her marriage to Ike Turner was all business and not romantic at all. She describes a wedding day that was devoid of joy and excitement, and a wedding night that was marred by an awkward and inappropriate incident. Through her story, Tina illuminates the less than ideal parts of her marriage to Ike, which stands in sharp contrast to her subsequent engagement to and wedding with Erwin Bach. The author looks back on her two nuptials and the changes she went through between the two marriages. Her first marriage was to Ike, and she says their wedding was a nightmare. She talks about the day Ike brought her to a sex performance in Tijuana just after their wedding. She complains about how miserable she is and can't understand how Ike could possibly be having fun there. When she tells the tale of their wedding to others, she glosses over this upsetting recollection and portrays it instead as a beautiful elopement. After describing her harrowing ordeal, the author moves on to describe her joyful engagement to her present spouse, Erwin Bach. She planned on having a lavish wedding straight out of a fairy tale, replete with a castle and all the trimmings. She enlists her florist friend, Jeff Latham, to assist make the landscape of Castle Algonquin more picturesque. In order to avoid stealing Erwin's thunder, the author forgoes the customary white wedding attire. She decides to wear a gorgeous Giorgio Armani gown instead, which she saw at a Beijing fashion show. She looks and feels like Cinderella in this outfit, which is constructed of green taffeta, black silk tulle, and Swarovski crystals. She creates a one-of-a-kind and individual wedding style by accessorizing with translucent black leggings and a beautiful black veil. Once again defying convention, the author chooses not to have bridesmaids and instead includes four young girls and one boy, all offspring of their friends, in the bridal party. She had Armani-designed gowns of varying hues made for them all. She thinks that little girls would be more important bridesmaids than grown women because of their innocence and grace. The author's best friend from the time they met in 1964, Rhonda Graam

, will be her maid of honor. Rhonda was originally an "Ike and Tina" fan and has remained a close friend throughout the series' run. Throughout Rhonda's life, the author highlights the importance of her commitment and friendship. The actions and occasions that occur just before a wedding. The unnamed narrator contemplates the meaning of their connections and the wedding day itself. They speak highly of Rhonda, who has been with them for almost fifty years in the roles of confidante, assistant, and tour manager. Rhonda is a link to the past for the narrator. The future, represented by their offspring, is also mentioned. Inviting only the closest of friends and family, the storyteller and their spouse, Erwin, meticulously craft a guest list. They make special arrangements for security and privacy because of the presence of famous people like Oprah and musician Bryan Adams. To protect their privacy from the prying eyes of the paparazzi, they erected a massive crimson screen—and with it, their cherished view of Zurich's lake. Famous florist Jeff Leatham is involved in the wedding preparations, and he goes above and above by creating an arrangement with more than one thousand roses in a wide range of colors. The narrator praises the flowers for their beauty and scent, but the stress of the planning causes them to check into a hotel. The narrator daydreams of taking an unexpected trip to Italy for their honeymoon. The narrator makes a passing reference, as the wedding day draws near, to the frequency with which brides and grooms argue and dispute. When it comes to creating a contingency plan in case of inclement weather, they disagree with Erwin. The narrator is set on not using a tent, thus he or she will not contemplate a backup plan. But they also find tent poles that someone brought along just in case. The narrator wants them taken out of the story. Workers begin erecting giant umbrellas to shield drones during the wedding, which presents an additional unanticipated problem. The narrator objects, since they would like not to have to rearrange their decorations. They walk away in annoyance, only to return after the umbrellas have been removed. They had hoped for a nice day for the wedding, but instead they got the hottest day of the year. Paper fans are given to each attendee to help them deal with the heat. The narrator says that they would rather use real fans than improvised ones. When it comes time to get ready for the wedding, the narrator and Erwin choose to host the other guests, notably the kids, in their house instead of the hotel. The narrator plays a crucial part in preparing the kids for the trip, and she presents them with commemorative Cartier bracelets. The kids will gather at the adjacent inn to wait for the ritual to begin. Reflects the narrator's thoughts on the relationships, wedding planning, and obstacles in the lead-up to the big day. It illustrates their desire for a stunning wedding and their will to be in charge of the proceedings despite whatever challenges they encounter. Companion, helper, and manager on the road; we'd been there for each other through thick and thin for over half a century. Rhonda represented the present, and the kids the future, for me. I was thinking something both familiar and fresh. Erwin and I invited our closest friends and family members after much deliberation.

Ever realistic, he cautioned that the wedding would draw a lot of attention due to the presence of superstars like Oprah and my old buddy, musician Bryan Adams. We had to erect a massive red screen to obscure our property from Lake Zurich, which meant I would have to spend the day without my favorite view of the lake. We didn't want the paparazzi to be able to peek in, so we couldn't look out. A personal best for Jeff Leatham. Freezer trucks from

Holland delivered over 100,000 roses in various colors of red, pink, orange, yellow, and white. I'd never seen flowers so gorgeous before, and their fragrance filled the air. The floral arrangements take days to make. Jeff had workers in the air and on the ground. Insanity is pervasive. There was no way somebody could have really lived there with all that chaos. So, Erwin and I settled into a room at Zurich's Dolder Grand Hotel, and I made daily trips there to monitor development. I had reached the point where I wanted to just forget about the whole wedding and start my vacation in Italy right immediately.

RETURNING TO THE FIRST STAGE

Despite being just 10 minutes from my house, I am now sitting in a dialysis chair in a hospital in Zollikon, Switzerland, as death taps me on the shoulder and says, "Tina... Tina, I'm here." While waiting eagerly for my body to be strong enough to receive my one possible salvation—a possibly life-saving kidney transplant—I am urgently striving to remain healthy, or as near to healthy as someone with 5% renal function can get.

Someone could remark, "Wait, I'm puzzled. Are you having a stroke or something?

Sweetheart, you have my confusion. Even I have trouble keeping track of all the medical disasters that have occurred in the four years since my wedding. The dangers of hypertension. Stroke. Cancer of the intestine. No! No! Poor sequence. Stroke. Der Schwindel, or vertigo, is the most common medical emergency in Switzerland, followed by colon cancer. Even worse, I've developed renal failure.

I'm going to need more than the customary "nine lives" to make it through this.

Several times a week, I have appointments at the clinic. Erwin's extreme caution and guardianship ensures that our daily schedule never changes. On days that I get therapy, he always arrives at the Château Algonquin at the same time and parks in a spot where I can go directly from the front door to the vehicle. Because he is such a gentleman, he has opened the door for the other passenger. After that, we take a short drive to a bakery in Küsnacht that's conveniently located near the station. To avoid being recognized, I wait in the vehicle while Erwin goes inside to get a selection of Swiss pastries. In this approach, we may ensure that we have something tasty to eat throughout the day.

Every visit to the doctor's office is like a stressful round of hide-and-seek. We have successfully kept my terrible illness a secret for numerous years. The Swiss have a far higher regard for personal privacy than their counterparts across the world, making this a realistic option. When I'm at the clinic, where I'm sure the paparazzi will be waiting for me, Erwin and I have a very specific system in place to make sure no one recognizes us.

Erwin takes a rear entry to park the car when we arrive. The dialysis units are conveniently located a short distance away. In the colder months, I like to conceal behind a black cloak or a thick coat with a big hat. So that no one can hear me and figure out that I'm speaking English, Erwin and I keep quiet on the walk in. I can't afford to have random people who see me snap pictures of me to sell to the press.

I'm not given a separate room since I'm not a diva and would be insulted if the staff did so. I don't want to be singled out because of the good fortune that has fallen upon me. The physicians are flexible with me since we both want to avoid being photographed. My visits are always arranged at times when there is less patient activity, and my space is separated from the rest of the hospital by a curtain.

I make an effort to enjoy my time in the chair. When I can stomach it, I eat the pastry while reading. My strange ritual is to always carry the same three books: The collection of Secrets by Deepak Chopra, The Divine Comedy by Dante, and a collection of photographs by the great Horst P. Horst. There should be nourishment for the soul, stimulation for the mind, and pleasure for the body. These novels never fail to make me reflect on who I am and what I believe in. They are a constant source of encouragement and motivation for me.

While having my blood cleansed, I do these procedures again every day. Drift as you read, dream, and wake up. Erwin has been on my mind. My late mother and sister, my kids, and my own upbringing keep playing through my head. And I can't believe I've been remembering Ike. Every time I think I've gotten away from it all, he comes back to get my attention. The early days, the terrible times, and my choice to leave him and begin a new life all come back to haunt me. Many of these ideas had crossed my head previously, but never with such clarity. This time, I'm trying to figure out the answers to my own questions. When you're staring mortality in the face, you reevaluate your life.

How did I end up in a dialysis chair instead of enjoying my fairytale wedding in a château on Lake Zurich? Quite a tale, indeed. How exactly did I go from Nutbush, Tennessee to this French chateau? That's a really lengthy one as well. Every moment I spend hooked up to the dialysis machine heightens my awareness of my own death. I can take as much time as I need. Now is the time to reflect on my life so far, to ask myself what all of this means for the here and now, and to wonder, Will I even have a future?

I think it's important for you to know my background so you can understand my narrative. It all started when I was born as Anna Mae Bullock on November 26, 1939. My whole life since then has been devoted battling the effects of negative karma. How did it feel to be an unloved baby? How was the kid's upbringing? How did that little girl manage to pull through when the odds were stacked against her?

Here, let me fill you in on the details.

My mother, Zelma Currie Bullock, who we nicknamed "Muh" (the first syllable of the word "mother"), was a constant presence in my life, but she was also a constant absence during the first few years of my life. She was a pampered brat as a kid and a spoiled brat now. Her father chose her above her three brothers, instilling in her the belief that she was worthy of everything she set her mind to. My dad, Floyd Richard Bullock, was a big part of her upbringing. Because she could, she snatched him away from another woman. That's how they met, which was a terrible idea from the start. My parents' marriage was fraught from the day they wed until my sister Alline was born. Then she discovered out she was pregnant with me just when Muh thought they should finally split up, so she stayed.

My mother was a childbearing lady, but she had no interest in having any of her children grow up to be as mischievous as I was. I was a complete opposite of Alline. I was the active tomboy who did anything she could to get Muh to notice her. I was able to see there was a difference between us very early just by observing how she interacted with my sister. I remember thinking, "That's nice," whenever I saw her gaze lovingly at Alline's face and caress her. If only she would do it to me, I'd be happy. Muh combed Alline's silky and delicate hair with a light hand. My time came, and she twisted and tugged furiously at my head since my woolly hair was not as attractive as Alline's and was much more difficult to comb. Maybe the fact that it was my made it more difficult for her.

Because Alline was better behaved than I was, my mother spared her the switch punishments I received. Muh thought I was too busy. Either I got into trouble or I was the one causing problems, so I was constantly trying to get away from mom and her switch. I would do everything, from fleeing under the bed to climbing a tree, to avoid being whacked with the sharp end of that stick.

That was the moment I realized my mom hated me. Now I'm curious as to whether or not she ever loved anybody save herself and perhaps Alline. To put it bluntly, she hated my dad. My first recollection is of my parents arguing. To be fair, Muh could hold her own in a fight, for better or for worse. She was a confident, capable lady who could handle herself in any situation. She would put a stool in front of the window and sit there, trying to figure things out. She was the one to go when she'd had enough, leaving behind everyone and anything she pleased.

When my mother left my brother and me, I was eleven years old. In 1950, Alline and I were in a similar predicament as when our parents left Nutbush for Knoxville after WWII in search of better career opportunities. However, they often requested our return, so we paid them a visit. It was different this time. I was a young, perplexed child. It was tough going to school. The going was rough. I really needed a mom. In a state of panic, I hurried around the house seeking for her. I walked up to the mailbox hoping to see a letter from Muh. My mother wanted to write to my father, but she knew that he would find out where she was hiding if she did. As soon as he learned where she was staying in St. Louis, he sent Alline and me to convince her to return home.

When she spotted me, she cooed, "Come here, baby." I don't know why she kept calling me baby. And so, I pondered. I never believed Muh when she attempted to be kind to me. I just did not believe her. I decided to maintain a safe distance. I avoided seeing her after she disappeared.

Now that I think about it, Muh and I were at odds with each other our entire lives, if not actively separated from one another. But it didn't stop me from being a responsible adult daughter and providing for her when I was financially stable enough to do so. No matter how contentious our relationship was, I always made sure she was comfortable and got good stuff. A psychic I saw in London in the late 1980s informed me, "You weren't wanted when you were born, and you even knew it when you were inside your mother." What I had suspected all along was verified by her.

Muh began sobbing as I gave her the psychic's prediction. The best she could come up with to justify herself was "I saved your life." When mother said she protected me from my father during an argument, she meant it literally. She didn't get away with it because of me. What I really said was, "I'll bet you're happy you did, Muh, because look where you are now!" Muh enjoyed being recognized as Tina Turner's mother more than anything else. In "saving" me, I wanted her to realize how much she benefited herself.

The fact that I didn't give up despite everything is miraculous, therefore I suppose you could say I was born with a Buddha nature. Despite growing up in a chaotic household and having a rocky connection with my mother, I was always a joyful, carefree, and optimistic person. "Where do you get such strength?" people often ask me. I often say that it's something I was born with. I've always been a confident, self-reliant person. It wasn't easy, but I was given the fortitude to make it through. My positive outlook has never failed me.

Besides not like my childhood job in the cotton fields, I have no regrets about my time spent growing up in Nutbush, a little community on Tennessee's Highway 19. I don't need it and thank you very much for asking. Our one-story, Southern-style shotgun home (named so because, according to urban legend, one could fire a pistol from the front door into the rear), was a pleasant place to relax. We were not among the impoverished. We had a bountiful harvest thanks to our sizable garden. We were a member of an engaging network of loved ones. Everyone was busy Monday through Saturday and spent Sunday at church.

My maternal grandmother, Mama Georgie Currie, was extremely kind and fun-loving, but my paternal grandmother, Mama Roxanna Bullock, was quite rigid. There was never any doubt in my mind that I'd rather hang out with Mama Georgie. Her home had a joyful, energetic vibe, in contrast to the strict, rule-bound environment of Mama Roxanna's.

I thrived on the independence that came with living in the country. My parents dropped me off at home and proceeded to work in the fields where my dad was the farm supervisor. I was a little kid who had to use a chair to reach the milk and cookies, but I was also old enough to amuse myself in less than ideal ways. I would climb any tree in sight without a second's hesitation. I sought for excitement and danger wherever I could find it. I gambled and can recall many close calls with death.

Every farm I visited appeared to have at least one horse who actively disliked human children. Even though we were warned not to go near there, my grandma's house was calling to me one day when I was sick of playing by myself. I believed I would be able to outwit that terrible horse. You know, those creatures have another sense, so I opened the door softly. He overheard my fumbling steps and quickly made his way in my direction.

The distance to Mama Georgie's home wasn't great, but to a little girl fleeing an aggressive beast, it seemed like an eternity. The horse had caught up to me and was ready to drag me down and trample me when I managed to reach the fence and start screaming. One of our billy goats, bleating like a Disney character, went over to distract the horse. My cousin Margaret swooped in at the last second and pulled me to safety as the horse turned its head away. What my dad did with the horse, I'll never know, but that goat was my best friend. I've always felt that he was the one who rescued me.

Outdoors was where I felt most at peace, despite the risks. When times are tough, kids learn to adapt. They discover a way to cope with the difficulty. Whenever I wasn't indoors, I was out in the yard or nearby fields, checking at the animals or staring at the sky. When my mother was living there, it was often a stressful one. When she departed, everything was sad. However, I found solace and peace in the great outdoors. When I went there feeling down and furious, it always helped me heal. When asked, "Where have you been all day?" Dreamy and untidy, I returned home to find out. When did I get here? No specific location; I simply felt better being outdoors.

Going to class was never something I looked forward to. The Flagg Grove School in Nutbush, like many other rural schools of the period, consisted of a single large room constructed of clapboard and shared by three classes. I was always terrified of getting called to the blackboard because of how poorly I performed in school. My math instructor called on me once as we were working on a problem in class. The panic began. I panicked because I didn't know what to do. Everyone in the room saw that I didn't know the answer, and I recall collapsing to the floor, kicking and weeping.

In retrospect, I believe my instructor should have done something, but back then, I doubt anybody really knew what a learning disability was, and I was most certainly one. All by myself, powerless, and ashamed, I felt. I wouldn't have used the word "embarrassed" back then; instead, I would have used the term "ashamed" to describe how I felt about myself as I stood there in front of the other students, tears obscuring the numbers in front of me. The capacity wasn't present in my head. I labeled it "not smart," and I suffered because I thought I had to conceal my idiocy from my loved ones and, later, my colleagues and superiors at work.

Later in adulthood, when I was more educated, I altered my mind about my learning disabilities when physicians explained why I struggled. My prefrontal cortex was involved. My imagination was on fire and working double speed, but my brain was not wired to be proficient in math or literacy. After hearing Princess Beatrice, Queen Elizabeth's granddaughter, explain her dyslexia in many interviews, I was able to overcome a deep-seated feeling of inferiority I'd carried with me my whole life. Although I am aware that others have discussed this issue, something about the manner she presented it caught my attention. She said she was dyslexic and unable to count, among other things. I might have been the one she was describing. I finally felt like I had some clarity about what was going on with me.

The Buddhists have a saying: "turning poison into medicine." That sums up what went on at Flagg Grove School, where I suffered several public shamings in front of my classmates and teachers. My great-grandfather, Benjamin Flagg, was the original owner of the land that provided the location for the school, according to research done by historian Henry Louis Gates in his PBS show African American Lives. To ensure that black children could attend school, he sold the property below its fair market value. That information really affected me.

The West Tennessee Delta Heritage Center eventually reached out to me a few years ago. The ancient Nutbush school was suggested to be relocated to neighboring Brownsville and converted into a Tina Turner museum. They planned this event to both honor my musical accomplishments and shed light on the experiences of African American students in the South throughout the 1940s. The school, abandoned for many years (it was converted into a barn), required extensive renovations. With the money we obtained, we were able to carefully renovate the building and fill it with Tina Turner artifacts at its new location. It was created to look like a cotton field outside the windows. In 2014, I built a museum where my childhood phobia of the blackboard was memorialized by displaying my childhood uniform and gold records on my original wooden schoolgirl desk. No longer does it frighten me. Now I'd like to believe it encourages others to triumph over adversity, transforming poison into medicine.

One part of me is the Anna Mae who sobbed in front of the class. Another Anna Mae, a natural performer, would have loved to be the center of attention and would have done everything to keep it. If only someone had stopped me right then and said, "Wait! Turn on the stereo! If I had seen it, I would have sprang to my feet, grin ear to ear, and started performing on the spot. I had zero trouble performing in front of an audience or receiving positive feedback afterward. I always felt I had superior singing ability than the other ladies around me, even when I was a tiny child. That ability is innate in me. My ability to utilize my voice effectively was my special talent.

I've always been a singer. When my parents first moved to Knoxville, I remember my mother bringing me shopping. Knoxville, in contrast to Nutbush, was a large metropolis with several shopping options. I was probably about four or five years old when the salesgirls discovered my hidden talent for singing and promptly seated me on a stool to listen to my renditions of today's top tunes. My first line, "I was walking along, singing a song," came out of my mouth without hesitation. When I heard a song on the radio, I would learn practically all of the lyrics immediately. It was as easy as a snake losing its skin to transition into a new one. This ability was innate in me. I was a small girl with a huge voice, and the salesgirls thought I was so amusing that they gave me a glass bank full of bright coins: dimes, nickels, quarters, and even fifty-cent pieces. My very first paying customers!

When we were in Knoxville, we attended services at the "sanctified church," which had its headquarters in the city. The fact that it was so different from the Baptist church I grew up in in Nutbush, even if I had no idea what the word "sanctified" meant, was fantastic. When the crowd was filled with what they termed the "Spirit," they began to sing, clap their hands, and dance joyfully. God and music had taken possession of them. They had me singing and dancing along with them. When everything picked up in volume and speed, it was almost like being in a performance. I was not familiar with the specifics of their faith, but I found the whole show quite interesting.

My loved ones in Nutbush served as an attentive audience. My mother had a kid before she met my father, so my half-sister Evelyn, my cousins, and I often put on impromptu performances at Mama Georgie's. There was never a moment when I didn't know exactly what to do or how to accomplish it whether it came to singing or dancing. I was the one who took the reins and led the group in music selection and choreography. Imagining ourselves onstage was a lot of fun. Alline, as an adult, decided she didn't like her appearance in the picture, so she burned it. The fact that it was the only photo I had of myself when I was thin and all voice made me feel terrible.

Singing during picnics was always a blast for me. While picnics were enjoyed by everybody, I found that the ones hosted by the black community in Nutbush were the most exciting and entertaining. Live music was provided by Mr. Bootsy Whitelaw, a local legend in this section of Tennessee. Another musician joined him on snare drum while he played the trombone. Those two were far more thrilling to me than a marching band would have been. My reputation as the "little Anna Mae" who sang with Mr. Bootsy quickly spread. Whatever songs he had me sing along to, I was right there by his side, trying to get the audience going wild with volume and enthusiasm. I invited the bystanders to join Mr. Bootsy in song. I was so inspired by Bootsy Whitelaw that I dedicated a song to him (entitled "Bop along, bop along, Mr. Bootsy Whitelaw") when I was in a band with Ike many years later.

Whenever I sang, I was always on the move. Whether it was a scripted step or not, I was constantly performing a little dance. Not even my sister could dance. My mom was not a good dancer. And yet, I could. In my opinion, singing and dancing go hand in hand.

When my living circumstances grew unstable and I was moved about often, I found great solace in singing as a means of expression and release. After Muh passed away, my father up and left the family when I was thirteen. After spending some time with our cousins, Alline and I moved home with Mama Roxanna, who kept a close eye on us. Connie and Guy Henderson, a young white couple, were a safe haven and a loving family to me and their infant. I felt at home at their beautiful home and honored to be included in their family. After going through so much change, I yearned for stability.

Because of their high standards, the Hendersons served as a great inspiration to me and my family. They showed me how to keep a beautiful house, which they had stocked with literature and art. They taught me how to behave appropriately. I was even taken out of my own state of Tennessee on a vacation to Dallas, Texas. They demonstrated to me that a married couple could be affectionate toward one another and coexist well with their young children. Although this kind of conduct may be the norm for some, I have never encountered it.

At fifteen, I had my first serious connection with Harry Taylor, a high school basketball star and my first true love. Harry was the ideal leader and student. He was attractive, well-liked, and captain of the football team. I thought we would eventually settle down and get married, so I put up with his erratic behavior—he would break up with me, meet another lady, and then come back—because I was so happy to be with him. When I first thought of this scheme, I was just fifteen years old. When Harry became pregnant by another girl and married her, it was the last straw for me. That type of disillusionment was not something I wanted to feel again any time soon.

I moved in with Mama Georgie in the hopes of starting again. Although no one appeared to care enough to challenge my judgments, I felt I was mature enough to do it on my own.

Mama Georgie passed away a few months later, while I was still sixteen and in high school. I had no notion what to do with myself without her. Following that, I accepted my mother's offer to go to St. Louis. We arrived, and Alline was already there. After being apart from Muh for so long, I was hesitant to move in with her, but the prospect of city life piqued my interest. I was no longer a helpless infant who required constant care from my mother. I felt more secure knowing that I could defend myself, at least in theory.

Muh leaving, my dear cousin Margaret dying in a car accident, Harry breaking my young heart by leaving me for another girl, Mama Georgie, and now the Hendersons; all people I cared about and had to say goodbye to.

To be honest, I never experienced love, therefore I stopped caring. Certainly not in my opinion. I suppose I managed to put up some kind of defense against it. Just because you don't care about me doesn't mean I have to stop living. I'll keep going even if you don't love me. Before I even realized what a mantra was, "I'll go on" was my constant thought.

I moved in with Mama Georgie in the hopes of starting again. Although no one appeared to care enough to challenge my judgments, I felt I was mature enough to do it on my own.

Mama Georgie passed away a few months later, while I was still sixteen and in high school. I had no notion what to do with myself without her. Following that, I accepted my mother's offer to go to St. Louis. We arrived, and Alline was already there. After being apart from Muh for so long, I was hesitant to move in with her, but the prospect of city life piqued my interest. I was no longer a helpless infant who required constant care from my mother. I felt more secure knowing that I could defend myself, at least in theory.

Muh leaving, my dear cousin Margaret dying in a car accident, Harry breaking my young heart by leaving me for another girl, Mama Georgie, and now the Hendersons; all people I cared about and had to say goodbye to.

To be honest, I never experienced love, therefore I stopped caring. Certainly not in my opinion. I suppose I managed to put up some kind of defense against it. Just because you don't care about me doesn't mean I have to stop living. I'll keep going even if you don't love me. Before I even realized what a mantra was, "I'll go on" was my constant thought.

A HANDS-ON HOLD has been taken on me

When I first moved to St. Louis, I felt a little confused and lonely in my new life. I was thus overjoyed when my attractive and sophisticated friend Alline offered to take me out to a club in racy East St. Louis. Ike Ike and the Kings of Rhythm played there nightly, and they always had a packed house. Without a doubt, I was familiar with them, as was everyone else. Although Ike's "Rocket 88," one of the earliest rock 'n' roll songs ever, was a huge smash, he made no money off of it due to the nature of the record industry at the time. In the St. Louis and East St. Louis area, Ike Turner was the most in-demand and dedicated performer. I was thrilled to finally see him perform at the Club Manhattan after reading about him in the press on a regular basis.

When I first saw Ike perform, he was dressed to impress in a sleek black suit and tie. Ike wasn't the type since he wasn't conventionally gorgeous (or even attractive). Keep in mind that I was only a schoolgirl of seventeen when I first laid eyes on a guy. Although he was just twenty-five at the time, Ike struck me as ancient due to his processed hair, diamond ring, and slender physique (he was all edges and sharp cheekbones). Never before had I seen somebody so skinny. God, he's ugly, was all I could think.

I was very certainly in the minority position. Women of all races found Ike attractive despite the inherent risk he posed. And Ike wasn't just threatening in appearance; he really was. The legend about the time he beat up someone with a pistol earned him the moniker "Pistol Whippin' " Ike Turner, and there were many others about his terrible temper, flare-ups with his bandmates, and confrontations with envious ladies (and occasionally their irate spouses). The fact that Ike Turner was a volatile individual with a notorious dark side added to his allure.

Ike was a popular figure despite his notoriety as a fugitive from the authorities. That guy was a lot of laughs. Flavors of the South. He may not have spoken perfect English, but that was just how he was. When he walked out on stage, he really set the place on fire. He plucked at his guitar or sat down at the keyboard and made it sing. The masses completely lost it. As I am. On the first night, I was moved to reply to a wonderful guitarist who was performing really thrilling music. Alline's boyfriend was in the band, therefore she often accompanied them to gigs. To accompany them, I pleaded with her. I started going to the Club Manhattan and other places where they played regularly with my sister acting as my chaperone.

Sometimes in between performances, Ike would ask a female from the crowd to come up and sing for the crowd. I aspired to be her. A dozen times, I saw myself bursting onto the stage, holding the microphone with the ease of someone who has done it their entire life, and belting out an unforgettable performance. But night after night, Ike chose other females who were more attractive and more sexually alluring than I was, but who couldn't hold a tune. I was simply "Little Ann," Alline's invisible younger sister, if he saw me at all.

Alline's boyfriend once attempted to get her to burst into song during a break. She rejected him outright, moving the microphone away from her. When I had the chance, I took it. Ike was performing "You Know I Love You" by B.B. King. My voice carried over the din and smoke and everyone, even Ike, turned to look at Little Ann again as I began to sing. The sound of my voice really threw him off. It sounded too strong to have come from such a frail little child. He was quite taken with what he heard that night, and it was the music itself that brought us together rather than the typical boy/girl or man/woman dynamic.

I was placed into a completely foreign setting. Imagine me: a teenager who is still, at heart, a country girl; naive and as eager as a puppy to please and be liked. Age wise, Ike had the upper hand. Lorraine was his current girlfriend (he probably had twenty, which just demonstrates how naive I am). We bonded quickly, more like siblings than romantic partners. His sizzling band, flashy pink Cadillac, and spacious East St. Louis mansion certainly made an impression. Muh, who didn't want me associating with the wrong crowd, even admitted that Ike had his own special kind of charisma.

The highlight was definitely the chance to pursue singing as a career. You could either sing along with the radio, sing in a church, or sing at a picnic with Mr. Bootsy Whitelaw if you were a singer in Tennessee. But this was the real deal: they were in a popular band and playing on a stage. Ike was the one who introduced me to music and even paid me to perform. We practiced and hit the clubs into the wee hours of the morning whenever we weren't on stage. We enjoyed one other's company immensely, and that was it.

Raymond Hill, a lovely young guy who was more my type than Ike, was there for me when I was in the mood for romance. He was one of the Kings of Rhythm's saxophone players and a resident at Ike's home. Sexual activity blossomed into a relationship, and soon I was expecting a child. Muh did not like it. Not to mention the fact that once Raymond fractured his ankle and went home to Clarksdale, Mississippi, that was the last time anybody saw him. It was just me. I had my first child, a son I called Raymond Craig, in 1958, when I was eighteen years old. I was healthy, resilient, and eager to start a new chapter in my life so that I could provide for my baby.

I considered nursing school off and on while working as a hospital assistant to help us out financially. What was I thinking? I relished feeling like a star when I put on the long gloves, dangling earrings, and beautiful outfits that Ike had purchased for me. There was a song within me that I needed to sing. This resulted in more time with Ike and more visits to his place, leading up to the night we finally went too far.

A gathering was held at Ike's place. One of the guys who was sleeping over made a remark about coming to my room later while I was there. My door didn't latch, so I remained with Ike for safety. That didn't happen very often. Innocently, during a sleepover, I had spent the night there before. This time we were sexually intimate by accident. This was to be expected from Ike. We both felt awkward and confused of what to do next, I believe. Seriously, I was a baby. Where was my wisdom? We just kept going instead of trying to mend fences and restore our relationship. My pregnancy with Ike's kid was finally confirmed in 1960.

It wasn't just that we had trouble with sex; it was just part of the issue. Looking back, I know that the day Ike realized that I was going to be his source of income was the day our relationship ended. He had planned to record "A Fool in Love," a song he had written for male vocalist Art Lassiter, but the two had a disagreement and never got around to recording it. Because Art couldn't make it in before the studio closed, I was asked to fill in on vocals. I put my own spin on the song. The protagonist of "A Fool in Love" is a lady who, ironically, falls in love with an abusive guy.

Indeed, the song's words, "You know you love him, you can't understand / Why he treats you like he do when he's such a good man," were prescient. Sue Records CEO Juggy Murray liked my rendition so much that he forked out $25,000 to acquire the rights and instructed Ike to make "that girl" the focal point of his performance.

What did Ike think when he heard that recommendation? The problems started when he tried to safeguard his interests.

Even now, many years later, I find myself trying to make sense of Ike. The longer I've been away from Ike and the older I become, the more vividly I can see him. Being at a safe distance allows for introspection, and I've been doing just that by attempting to understand his actions and rationalizing them away by telling myself, "Oh, that's why he did what he did."

Ike's problems, like mine, started right from birth. He had arrived from vengeful and combative Clarksdale, Mississippi. He saw his father's long, agonizing murder at the hands of white guys who intended to teach him a lesson for playing about with a white lady when he was a young child. Ike buried his animosity and never let it out.

Later in life, he struggled academically. Because he was unattractive, kids picked on him relentlessly. Because he was so much fun to play with, girls would meet him behind the school building, but they would never be seen with him in public. That made him furious and hateful on top of everything else. His success would serve as his payback. He told himself, "One day I'll have a big car and all the women I want." He'd go to any lengths to achieve his goal.

After spending more time with Ike and seeing his behavior away from the spotlight, I came to the conclusion that he had not had a good education. The schools I had attended had intellectual instructors and children from decent households, so I could recognize the difference. Since my parents had just passed away and I was staying with either my grandparents or the Hendersons, I had to take the bus in, but I was fortunate enough to be around by intelligent people and learn by observation.

I used every second wisely while I was in school. I used to be a choir member. The basketball squad included me. A former cheerleader here. The professors appreciated anything I had. They were always there to protect and care for me. And I was open to their suggestions when they were made. I've been doing this since elementary school when the librarian instructed us to do so to improve our posture. The principal told me he was expecting me to behave well, so I promised that I wouldn't let him down. I strove to learn the optimal procedure so that I can develop and advance.

Ike was never given the chance. He probably didn't get beyond the fifth grade, and he had an inferiority complex stemming from the fact that he always came across as clueless, even when he was absolutely correct. A lot of his aggression stemmed from his insecurity over his social ineptitude and lack of formal schooling.

But Ike was also very gifted musically and had what we termed street smarts. Ike's musical prowess and unrelenting drive allowed him to purchase a luxury vehicle, a mansion, and an endless supply of women. He even had a number one single. Then he paused, and the rage and fury returned when he realized he wasn't going to go any farther.

When it became clear that "A Fool in Love" would be successful, Ike had an idea: he rebranded the Kings of Rhythm as the Ike and Tina Turner Revue in the hopes of reaching a wider audience. If the new revue was to be successful, however, Ike would need to own me financially and emotionally so that I would never leave him. The financial aspect was simple to complete. Ike was not a vocalist. He wanted to make it big in show business, but I was his only chance. He reasoned, "Okay, I'll change her name and call the group the Ike and Tina Turner Revue—that puts me right there in the title, so she doesn't exist without me." He recalled a TV show character named "Sheena," and he liked that my new first name rhymed with her name. My new surname, "Turner," also gave the false impression that we were married. Ike was constantly planning ahead. He had the name "Tina Turner" trademarked, so I couldn't use it.

What does it matter if we call it something else? Everything. I became Ike's property with those two words.

Ike used a variety of strategies to keep me under his mental thumb. He took advantage of my good intentions by pleading with me to be faithful to him before our relationship got physical. Hangdog as he was, he informed me that whenever he made a successful song for someone, they eventually dumped him. As a token of my appreciation for everything he had done for me—after all, if Ike loved you, he would give you the shirt from his back—I made a pact with him to never, ever abandon him. I've never been one to tell a falsehood as far back as I can remember. It's simply how I roll. What I stated was what I intended. What was promised was what was promised, period. My word to Ike was important, and I fully planned to honor it.

However, Ike had no faith in me. In reality, Ike had no faith in humanity. He sought assurance that I wouldn't back out of my word, so he used a different tactic to keep me bound to him: terror. I should have listened to my gut when he first suggested the new Ike and Tina Turner concept and said I needed a better stage name. I was young and naive back then. I had the nerve to challenge him, explaining that I had second thoughts about his proposed tour and that I didn't want to alter my name. His first attack was rhetorical. I was getting the brunt of Ike's cruel tongue. Then, wanting to teach me a lesson I wouldn't soon forget, he grabbed up a wooden shoe stretcher and walked toward me.

Ike was totally on the ball. Guitarists know better than to use their fists in a quarrel, since their hands are their most valued instrument. He shielded his hands and hit me over the head with the shoe stretcher, which hurt like hell since you're supposed to hit people over the head. I was so taken aback that I began to weep. Although my parents battled often, I had never seen my father so severely punish my mother. I had no prior experience with this, so I was still trying to make sense of it all. What happened next was the last thing I anticipated. Ike lowered the litter and told me to get into the bed. What happened was terrible. At that very moment, I became deeply antagonistic toward him. Making love, if you could call it that, was the last thing I wanted to do. After he was done, I laid there with a throbbing head, thinking, "You're pregnant and you have nowhere to go."

Ouch, you've really messed up this time. That night, Tina Turner entered the world, while "Little Ann" vanished into obscurity.

It was Ike, not Tina, who acted like the showbiz heavyweight in the early days of the Ike and Tina Turner Revue. In reality, I was Cinderella—a slave girl. Me, Ike, and the band, plus the "Ikettes," a trio of female vocalists who accompanied me, made up the revue. When I became pregnant, I hid my growing belly behind a maternity girdle (I was slender enough that it didn't show) and embarked on my first exhausting, multi-city tour, leaving baby Craig in St. Louis with a sitter.

You have no idea the state those early clubs were in, particularly the black ones. They lacked facilities for changing clothes. If we were fortunate, we'd have access to a storage room or a closet, and even then, we'd have to clear it out first. To do our makeup, we set up our own mirrors, perched on our little Samsonite luggage or a keg in the absence of seats, and prayed for electricity. There were no restrooms available. We'd use a bottle with the top lopped off and then take it outside to dispose of it. After we had paid our dues and moved up to the white clubs, things improved, but not by much.

It was all on us since Ike was so tight with his money. He was quite stern. Despite his natural tendency toward recklessness and indulgence, Ike insisted on having complete say over every aspect of the revue. He penalized the performers, including musicians and dancers, for the slightest indiscretions. If someone tore a stocking, was late to a practice, or said anything disrespectful, he would issue a 10 dollar punishment. One disgruntled Ikette even claimed that she owed more to Ike than she had earned. Someone inquired as to whether or not I was exempt from punishment for rule violations. You just heard a joke. Since I wasn't being paid, there was no need to fine me. When Ike was in a very giving mood, all I received was a roof over my head, food to eat, and a few nice items.

This is why I was unable to develop into a diva. No one ever gave me anything while I was growing up. My outlook was to never whine about adversity, but rather to embrace it and go on. Just make the most of the situation you're in, good or bad.

The Ikettes and I made the most of every situation and enjoyed ourselves immensely. Because we were always moving, our friendship became the one constant in our lives. It seemed like we were sisters. Because Robbie Montgomery, one of the original Ikettes and now the owner of the renowned soul food restaurant Sweetie Pie's, knew Ike never paid me, she would often give me money. Knowing I could count on her no matter what meant the world to me.

Dancing with the females was always a blast, and it would often be the highlight of my day. We put in many hours of practice, even in the automobile, perfecting our choreography by creating new routines or adapting existing ones. As in, "(Sham, Ba, Ba, Ba, Freeze, Freeze, Turn! (You go ahead and ascend, and I'll wait here for you when you return.) Our hallmark move, "The Pony," was inspired by a woman riding a pony and hails from a source I can't recall. The woman sits, and the pony prances about, using his legs in various ways. Like Michael Jackson's subsequent Moonwalk, the Pony was a traveling stride for us, keeping us on the move across the stage. We had a great time when Ike turned up the volume on the music. The usual refrain was "Oh, ho, it's on the track tonight." We had a blast showing off our skills to the crowd, and I think the audience would agree that it takes a skilled dancer to move so fast.

We had a great time just deciding on a "look." We learnt via trial and error that skirts and short dresses were best for drawing attention to our long, lean legs. Having a good dressing area made it much easier to keep up with a hairdo while on the road. My relationship with my hair has always been fraught, even from a young age. My hair was too large and woolly to keep in braids, so I took them out. As I grew older, I had it straightened, which required me to spend a long time in a chemically saturated beauty parlor having a stranger yank at my hair until the kinks were gone. There was no use in waiting around for processing to finish. Black hair, when touched when a person is singing, dancing, and sweating, will immediately return to its original state.

My first wig was the result of a mishap that ended up being a fortunate turn of events. My hairdresser left the bleach on my head for a bit too long when I went with the Ikettes to have our hair done. I had a gig that night and my over-processed hair began to come out and break. A wig was the only option for covering up the damage. It saved my life, but what I liked most about the wig was how it made me appear; the way the hair flowed when I moved; the way it was straight and lovely and stayed in place no matter what I did.

This occurred in the early 1960s, when wigs still looked crude and had thick, heavy, and harsh hairstyles. I learned how to alter the wigs so they would seem more natural since I didn't want to look like I was wearing a curtain of synthetic hair. The first step in getting the style perfect was for me to thin down the hair in strategic areas. Wefts, or little sections of excess hair, were then stitched on with a needle and placed where I felt they would provide the most volume. I invested in high-quality hair and, after much shaping and style work, my wigs quickly became the industry standard. We'd wear them on stage, then wash and set them afterward so they'd be fresh for the following day's performances.

Ike gave me complete freedom in that regard, although he did have final say on the soundtrack. Despite my inexperience, I had my own thoughts on how to best use my voice in performances. I had songs I was excited to perform, and some I was dreading. To give you an example, jazz isn't really my thing. I was raised on country and western and later came to appreciate the work of great female vocalists like Faye Adams and LaVern Baker. My favorite song by Baker was "Tweedle Dee." Both Mahalia Jackson and Sister Rosetta Tharpe were among my favorite musical artists. Those gospel singers had some serious pipes! And they were really commanding in appearance.

I didn't have a "girl" voice like most of the prominent female artists of the period, so I drew inspiration from male artists instead. Sam Cooke was my favorite of all time. In 1960, I was fortunate enough to see one of his performances at the Howard Theater in my hometown of

Washington, D.C. He was the most handsome black guy I'd ever seen, even more so than my high school lover Harry.

I accompanied one of the Ikettes to his concert, and it was standing room only. Sam Cooke stood there, shirt open, in a sharply fitted european suit, singing. He had always let nature take its course when it came to his hair. He was so hip and fantastic, singing, "Darling, you send me." I was really captivated. Walking toward the platform, I was suddenly pulled back by the girl I was with, who said, "Bullock [they nicknamed me Bullock], I will murder you! Where are you going? There was complete and utter chaos. The first artist I ever saw who could do it was Sam Cooke. When they heard his voice, they immediately softened.

A couple of years later, I was able to meet him in person in a Miami hotel. He approached me as we were all lounging by the pool. It took me by surprise when I learned that Sam Cooke knew me; to be honest, I'm not even sure if he recognized me; maybe he was just being kind. You know how some folks can just tell when you're feeling down? I was feeling down at the time—probably because Ike was up to no good—so Sam Cooke's thoughtfulness meant a lot to me. Later, I learned of his untimely passing. Ike broke the news of his murder to me. I'm grateful for the time we spent together and continue to remember him and his stunning voice.

I was a big Ray Charles fan. He could have the crowd going wild with his rendition of "What'd I Say" by the Raelettes. When he entered the stage, the crowd would immediately begin dancing and kicking. He possessed a different kind of "soul." Not your typical church soul music. He carried all of his possessions with him to the planet. Ray Charles was really one of a kind.

Numerous black performers at the period displayed originality in their art. Otis Redding, he spoke of his pain in songs like "The Dock of the Bay." I also saw James Brown at the Apollo. The crowd went wild when he performed the Mashed Potato (which I stole from him) on stage with his cute little bow legs. For the first time, I saw a black guy wearing a bright green jacket. Everyone, including myself, was profoundly moved by his presence. The crowd was essentially groveling at his feet.

There was something unique about each of these performances that I'm describing to you. The white audiences they attracted were so impressed that they abandoned pop music forever. They took inspiration from what African Americans were doing, and that style later influenced other musical genres.

As my taste in music evolved via exposure to these legends, I began to dislike Ike's direction for my vocal performance. His preferred style of delivery included a lot of "Hey, Hey, Heying" and growling, making him seem like he was preaching. I wanted to be able to utilize my voice in a manner that was more expressive and melodious, but I wasn't.

Looking back, I see that many of our disagreements sprang from my dissatisfaction with the roles he had envisioned for me to play. The experts labeled our disagreements "artistic differences." There was no way I could have told him, "I don't like that song" or "I don't want to deliver it this way." However, his intelligence was undeniable. He understood my emotions just by looking at me, and he was offended when I disagreed with him. "Miss Bullock," he would yell at her in a condescending tone. It's time to "get out there and sing the song." When I voiced my disagreement with him once, he spat in my face.

There wasn't much room for contemplation of what may have been. Due to Ike, we were much too preoccupied to worry about such a thing. Traveling, practicing, and performing became a never-ending cycle, and any downtime was filled with impromptu recording sessions. For me, the most memorable concert was our August 1960 performance at the Apollo Theater in New York City. One very large bridge stands out in my mind. When I first saw the cityscape, I exclaimed, "New York!" What a stunning city New York was back then. The sun was more dazzlingly golden than before. I wasn't familiar with the thoroughfares, but I'd never seen anything like the skyscrapers here. They seemed to reach heavenward, upwards, skyward. New York had everything: towering buildings with shining windows, honking horns, women in high heels (not shoes, as nowadays), scarves, and white gloves, and hot dogs from pushcarts. Seeing it in person was a once-in-a-lifetime opportunity that surpassed even the best movie.

At the Apollo, the crowd was enthusiastic, and the company was excellent. That night's comedy was a young Flip Wilson. Ike was nervous during the performance due of my constant movement and my advanced pregnancy. He attempted to reign me in by saying, "You'd better stop doing this or that," but I twisted and did the Pony all the way up until I gave birth in October. Because I was expecting a son and my tummy was pointed (exactly as the old ladies said), I wore clothes that covered up as much skin as possible. I felt secure in my straight, form-fitting underdress, and the flowy chiffon overdress helped me hide the "bump." Because of my tender age, I have an abundance of vitality and strength. During my whole pregnancy, I felt fantastic.

I don't know whether it was the adrenaline of performing on stage at the Apollo or just the fast-paced nature of the music, but at one point during the show I leaped down into the pit. The fact that no one could tell I was in the eighth month of my pregnancy is a testament to how well I dressed. That must have made everyone very anxious. But there was never any threat to the infant. The drop wasn't really that high, and I've always been quite athletic. I had confidence in my own abilities to deal with the situation.

We stopped in St. Louis on the way back across the country to see how Craig was doing while still staying at Ike's place with a sitter. Seeing him hurt so much. He was so little that he had just learned to speak. My baby just wanted to be hugged, and Ike wouldn't let him sit on my lap. He considered that a sign of weakness. When I returned later, Craig was sobbing uncontrollably in his bed. I comforted him by holding him in my arms. The following day, after we had already departed, he started yelling my name all over the place, "Ann, Ann," as if he were desperately trying to find me. He reflected on his mother's unconditional affection. When she was away from him, he always felt a void. Ann was missed. Ann, the person I used to be before Ike made things so difficult, was someone I missed, too.

I REFUSE TO BATTLE

Our nonstop traveling schedule didn't allow us much time at home. Ronnie, our kid, was nearly born when we were on our first tour. We were on our way to a Los Angeles hospital to perform at a few shows when Ike realized I was in labor. He thought I would have the kid and then go back to work immediately. I gave birth two days before going on stage to perform, and it was if nothing had happened. The truth was that there would be no concert and hence no money if I didn't sing.

This always leaves me scratching my head. I can't help but wonder why Ike was so cruel to me. That might have been a line from one of Ike's songs, only it really happened. He certainly wasn't making any logical decisions. If he had treated me with kindness, care, and respect, I may have stayed. Didn't it make perfect sense? I almost fell in love with him. At first, yes. And if we had worked together in a more professional manner, we might have achieved the success that was so vital to him, much like the famed duet Mickey & Sylvia. However, Ike was always a threat to himself. Everything of value was destroyed by him. He was unable to resist.

Now that I look back, I can see that our relationship was nothing like a "normal" one; it was characterized by abuse and terror rather than love and compassion. We pretended to be a happy couple by engaging in stereotypical activities. Together, we started a family. Ike packed us all up and drove us to Los Angeles, where he leased a home and we all lived together like a modern-day Brady Bunch: Ike Jr. and Michael, Ike's boys with Lorraine, grew up with Craig and Ronnie. At age 23, I became "Mother" to four little boys, aged two to four. Then, in 1962, we tied the knot in a gloomy Tijuana civil ceremony.

We had wonderful weather, clear sky, and palm palms where we were staying in Los Angeles. However, Ike's life was everything from tranquil. When we were in town, he insisted on setting up a recording studio in the living room, where he stayed up late every time. As it was, I was incapable of maintaining my vigil. Aw, man, they would have rushed me to the emergency room! On occasion, he would ask me in a very serious tone, "Tell me, what do you do for me?I wanted to blurt out, "Everything; singing; cooking; cleaning; and whatever else I have to do around here;" but I refrained, instead wondering how on earth I would make it through the day.

Both being at home and on the road has its drawbacks. I felt terrible since we were gone from the house more often than we were home, which was bad for the kids. After our first trip, Ike kept us so busy that we had bookings between our reservations. The band members would ride in our bus, and Ike, me, and, most likely, a mistress, would follow in Ike's Cadillac Brougham, which had a safe installed in the trunk.

Visiting far-flung destinations like New York and London, which I had only read about, was the best part of my travels. My family and I seldom went anywhere else to see our relatives, and because they all resided in close proximity, these visits were never very far. Due to the limited size of our social group, my father was able to track down my mother after she went missing by asking people she knew whether they knew anybody in Chicago, Detroit, or St. Louis. But because to the Ike and Tina Turner Revue, I got to travel the globe. Ike kept us too busy to go sightseeing or visiting museums, so I never had the chance to be a tourist. But I saw how others lived, and I picked up some useful pointers.

I wish I could have missed out on one region of the globe. It was difficult for us to go in the Deep South in the 1960s due to the high probability of encountering hostile racial circumstances. I can't count the number of times I overheard something like this: "We're driving through Mississippi, and a white police officer notices that we're black, and he signals for us to pull over." To one of our singers and drivers, Jimmy Thomas, he would remark, "Hey, boy," which was meant to be sexually suggestive. Is it true that you were speeding a little in this area?Jimmy would calmly respond, "No, sir, I was doing the speed limit." Then the cat-and-mouse game would start in earnest.

That's not what my meter says," the cop would reply. I have to take you in, I'm afraid.

For Jimmy, this would be the perfect opportunity to explain, "Sir, you know, we're singers and we're a little bit late. Do you mind if we handle this with you?"

The exchange of currency was inevitable. The cop got a raise and went home in his new car. And off we went, driving to our next assignment. ..until the following time we were stopped by the police. If the cops ever stopped us on the way to a gig, master negotiator Jimmy would have me and Ike come out and sing to prove to them that we were professional performers.

In 1964, when Rhonda first began working for us, we had to be cautious while going through the South, since the mere presence of a white lady in the company of a black band was enough to elicit hostile reactions. Sometimes, when we had a white bus driver or guitar player, Rhonda would sit next to him. When we ran out of petrol in a particularly unfriendly area, we once had to hide Rhonda's presence by having her lie on the floor of the vehicle while we refueled.

It was stressful to drive, but much more so to dine out anywhere than on the black side of town. Even a peaceful supper might quickly escalate into a life-threatening situation. I'll never forget the night we were in a restaurant and the waitress phoned the cops on us just because we were a bunch of black people. When she began shouting that I was a "black bitch," I sprang to my feet despite Ike's attempts to keep me down, and I responded, "But I'm a pretty black bitch." After a late concert, we'd often avoid the issue by heading to the next Greyhound bus station for some food. The meal wasn't particularly tasty, but at least it was safe.

When we weren't doing shows on the fly, which left us with little time to rest in between appearances, we stayed at well-known hotel and motel chains, and we always made sure to bring telegrams verifying our bookings. When you first drew up to a Holiday Inn, you could see the level of activity inside thanks to the open curtains and central light in each room. Sometimes, though, we would arrive at a hotel with confirmed bookings in hand, only to be informed that the property was "full" despite its apparent vacancy. The fact was that they actively discouraged black guests, particularly black musicians.

Rhonda, a headstrong young lady, would not take "no" for an answer. Occasionally, she'd go ahead and check in at the hotel on her alone before the rest of us arrived. Eventually, she got through to someone at corporate and explained the situation, saying that we had encountered bias at a few of their sites. From that point on, the hotel respected our bookings or Rhonda would have the hotel manager in hot water with the owner.

At times, we simply had to remain in the vehicle or on the bus since our itinerary was so jam-packed. It was great to sleep on the grass in the summertime. We tried all we could think of to get by till the next performance. A permanent state of mobility was achieved.

Ike's tactic was to keep me close to him, to make me feel tiny, whether we were on the road or back in L.A. (at this time, Ike had acquired a home on Olympiad Drive in the neighborhood of View Park). I wouldn't know who I was or where I fit in the world if he kept me in the "Ike and Tina" bubble with his little group of followers. In 1966, when I was at a low point in my life, the chance to record "River Deep—Mountain High" presented itself to me. How honored I felt when famous record producer Phil Spector reached out to Ike about collaborating with me is beyond words. Not knowing anything about him, but being encouraged by someone other than Ike, felt great. Naturally, Ike's first reaction was "No way," but then he saw yet another avenue to use me financially. When it came to me, he always acted like a pimp. Not a street-level pimp, but a pimp all the same. It was after Ike stated "Pay me first" to Phil that he was able to borrow twenty grand. Yet Phil was a bright guy. He had no interest in dealing with Ike or the problems that he brought. Tina alone. Phil demanded I come to his Hollywood home by myself to begin composing the tune.

I was eager to experiment with new songs and even a new vocal technique. I wanted to make the most of my independence since I seldom got the opportunity to travel alone back then. I made an effort to seem appropriate. I like to believe I've always had a strong eye for fashion, so this was a great opportunity for me. Miniskirts and bell bottoms were all the rage, and they fit my thin frame well. One of my fantastic Tina wigs gave me long, straight hair, and I donned a white blazer with matching leggings.

Hidden away on La Collina Drive, just off Sunset, was where Phil kept his house. I took a quiet lane that went to a courtyard with a huge fountain, apprehensive since I didn't know what to anticipate. There was no response when I knocked on the door. I pulled it open and stepped into a huge, old Hollywood-style room with a winding staircase and massive, antique European furnishings. What the heck, I thought to myself, still completely alone, this is quite strange. A voice surprised me; it turned out to be a mynah bird instead of a human being shouting, "Someone's here!" It was a scene straight out of Alice in Wonderland, when Alice goes down the rabbit hole, and I was Alice.

I took a seat, crossed and uncrossed my legs, and waited as the mynah bird resumed its internal monologue. Phil and I hadn't spoken before—Ike had arranged everything—but when he came jumping down the stairs, I remembered seeing this leprechaun-like guy at the bars where we played. He was constantly off to the side, hiding behind an odd hat. No cap was worn that day, only a wild crown of crinkly hair that protruded in every direction and made me think of the crazy scientists from the horror films I adored as a kid. He wore a T-shirt and pants, and I saw that his bare feet were startlingly white. He said, "Hello, Tina, I'm Phil Spector," and sounded quite erudite in his introduction.

We made our way to the living room's grand piano, where he sat down to play "River Deep—Mountain High," the tune he'd been saving for me. I mistook his gesture as a cue for me to start belting out the tune, so I began singing, "When I was a little girl I had a rag doll," in my best Ike impression. Phil cut me off abruptly, saying, "No, no, not like that—just the melody." Just the melody? I gave him full-on Tina, loud and passionate. Oh my goodness, I thought, this is fantastic! I still remember how liberating it felt to have a fresh outlet for my voice. I felt like doing a happy dance or running around shouting, "Woo hoo!"'

Learning about music was a perk of working with Phil. He always said the same thing whenever I went to practice there, eliminating any hint of Ike from my act. There was a noise in Phil's mind. He insisted that I not deviate from the melody in any way, shape, or form, and instructed me to sing it precisely as he had envisioned it.

The weird thing was, as soon as I left Phil, I couldn't recall a single lyric of the song, despite its eeriness. I probably blocked the thought out of my mind because I knew Ike wouldn't like it and I was frightened he may punish me with a beating, as he normally did when anything made him upset. I couldn't get the tune out of my brain since it was so unlike anything I'd ever played. ..until one Saturday night on the way home after a club date with Ike. Instantly, the song's refrain, "And I'll love you just the way I loved that rag doll," came flooding into my mind, and I began singing it in

Phil's style. Ike listened with a blank expression. True to my suspicions, the music he was exposed to was not his kind.
Saying, "So that's it, huh," he seemed to reject it. I could tell even as he was talking that he was planning some way to alter the vocals to make them sound more "Ike and Tina," which would have been disastrous. However, he couldn't get out of it. From conception to completion, Phil Spector was responsible for this. Ike had already been compensated, so he couldn't complain.
The longer I was with Phil, the more I came to the conclusion that he was, to put it mildly, out of the ordinary. There were things he did that just seemed odd to me. ..such as when he ate an apple that he had picked up off an ashtray. It was coated in ashes, so I didn't see why he did it. The thought that "Oh, he's so busy at the studio" caused me to ignore it. After spending so many hours perfecting that song, we all went a little bit insane from tiredness. At the time, I didn't realize that Phil had always been a little off his rocker.
We'd meet at Gold Star Studio every day, where Phil would drop as much on a single track as most record labels would on an entire album. I must have sang the first line a thousand times before we got to "And it gets stronger every day," but Phil was still unsatisfied. There was no clear indication of when I was succeeding or failing. I'm human, and I may be a little naive at times. I was sweating profusely and could think of nothing except the urge to cool down and dry off. Is it okay if I take my shirt off?" I enquired. During the midst of the take, I took off my shirt and continued singing. The studio audience's response, however, was larger than Ben-Hur, even though I was

wearing a bra. Tina removed her top. Just do whatever it takes to get through that song, I told myself. I'm still confused about his motivations. I have no idea whether or not I won his approval. But I kept trying nevertheless.

In addition, I was musically illiterate; Ike never spoke to me about music, so I had no idea what the "Wall of Sound" was or who Phil Spector was. One day I dropped by the studio and was taken aback to see a full orchestra and a choir (yes, a choir) of backing singers. Just a girl from Tennessee who fell in love with Ike and decided to pursue music full-time. I had never, ever seen anything like that before. OK, Tina," Phil finally said.I made an effort to hide my anxiety. When I got into the studio and began singing, the orchestral strings, horns, and drums all converged on me. I contributed by using my voice as an instrument.

Phil claims that no one else, not even Darlene Love or the Ronettes (who both have great vocals), has been able to sing "River Deep—Mountain High" correctly. He probably picked me because I can reach high notes without resorting to falsetto, which is what most vocalists do. But in my regular speaking voice, I can sing octaves higher and hold my own against an orchestra. Phil had been keeping an eye on me every time I went out to the club. He had heard my voice and liked what he heard, so he asked me to sing his song. Before then, I was singing in the style of my mentor and producer, Ike. The other ability I knew I possessed all along. I was curious about its existence and decided to look into it. My mind was blown by this song's message. I was relieved, energized, and eager to try my singing chops at other genres. Never in all my years of performing have I ever skipped performing it. That wouldn't fly with the crowd.

It was expected that "River Deep—Mountain High" would be a smash success, but to our surprise, the American public didn't take to it. When pushed, the DJs said that they weren't sure how to play it since it didn't sound "black" enough to be rhythm and blues or "white" enough to be pop. Things were different in England. The song became a huge hit in that region. As a result of its immediate success, the Rolling Stones asked the Ike and Tina Turner Revue to serve as the tour's opening act in the United Kingdom.

Our first trip to Europe confirmed my ideal way of life, just as "River Deep—Mountain High" had done for my ideal method of singing. London in 1966 was the epicenter, the point where everything suddenly exploded. And of course, there's Carnaby Street, where all the "mods and rockers" call home. I felt like I was living in a fairy tale at times. The double-decker buses, the little black taxis, and the charming white townhouses lined the streets, all of which I found quite appealing. The hotel we stayed at on Cromwell Road was the Norfolk, and every day at 6 a.m. The sound of horses trotting toward Buckingham Palace for the Changing of the Guard roused us from our sleep. Wimpy's, the English equivalent of McDonald's, was the only establishment open after the play ended, although it had more character than the McDonald's back home. London had nice hamburgers, too, but the locals looked at us like we were from another planet when we asked for iced tea. You're asking for trouble by ordering "iced" hot tea. That's what an American is like, they sneered.

It was like being transported to another universe for a girl from Nutbush and St. Louis. Like falling in love at first sight, I instantly felt at home in this city and among its inhabitants. Still, I had no desire to return to the United States. I really considered staying! When I first visited France and Germany, I had a similar reaction. These exotic locales may have been homes of past incarnations. Believer in reincarnation? Me, definitely.

The Royal Albert Hall holds over 5,000 people, so when the Stones played there, the place was filled to the gills with fans eager to see the band. Never before have we played for such a large crowd. From behind the curtain, Ike said, "I want Ike and Tina, just Ike and Tina to fill this place," which was a ridiculous wish. We were anxious, but it was unwarranted. We were a hit with the audience, and the Stones agreed. We really floored them with our dance moves. Mick claimed that we had the crowd amped up and excited before the Stones appeared on stage, making them work harder to outdo us. That's real teamwork: when the support act and the main act feed off one other to produce something fresh and exciting for the audience.

With a hundred things to do before our performance of "Cinderella" at the Albert Hall, I spent most of my time backstage. The first time I saw Mick Jagger, he was waiting in the wings, and the first thing I noticed was how white his face was. He came to the Ikettes' and my shared dressing room later and stated, in his distinctive voice, "I like how you girls dance." We'd seen him before, when he was a bit more awkwardly parading about with his tambourine on stage. We felt it was sweet that he was impressed by our dancing, so we invited him to join us and showed him the

Pony. Mick learned the moves quickly, although he struggled with some of the choreography. Not deterred, he gave it another shot on the following episode, and the results made us exclaim "Well, that's good." Never once did he give me or the ladies any credit for teaching him his new moves. Mick often reflects on his mother's influence, remarking, "My mother taught me how to dance." My response is, "Okay. No problem there. But I'm not stupid.

My visit to a psychic in England sparked what would become a lifetime interest in the paranormal for me. I'm always on the lookout for advice. At the conclusion of that first reading, the psychic surprised me with a revelation. She predicted that you'd make it to the top tier of Hollywood stars. A friend or lover may drop from your life like a leaf from an autumn tree, but you'll pick yourself up and keep moving on. There couldn't be a Tina without Ike, or so I thought. Nonetheless, I filed away the concept and reflected on it through trying times. And each day they became more severe.

Walking a tightrope while sharing a home with Ike. My words and my gaze toward him needed to be carefully considered. Once you unchained him, he would pounce on anything, only to fight; he was constantly on edge, ready to fight like a dog. I didn't have a car or even a little allowance of $5, so I was stuck there. I had to resort to stealing $20 from the roll Ike carried in his wallet whenever I needed money. When he was in a good mood, he'd take me shopping because he believed that if I looked well, it reflected well on him. In a twisted sense, the black eyes, cracked lips and ribs, and swelled noses I received from Ike were marks, a proof of ownership, and yet another manner in which he said, "She's mine and I can do whatever I want with her."

I had to get out of here, but I had no idea what to do first. I made a disastrous attempt at escape once. Since I was stuck, I decided to take a bus to St. Louis and see Muh. It didn't take Ike long to figure out where I was going; he met me at a bus stop on the way and demanded that I turn around. Something went wrong there. When I was at my lowest, I thought that suicide was my only option. And I had no problem with leaving since I saw no need to continue living that way. I really considered ending my own life. What caused me to lose it on a normal day in 1968? To begin with, there were three ladies there, and Ike was engaging in sexual activity with each of them. We had three Anns in the group. That's not anything anybody could have made up. There was just one name he needed to remember.

Ann Thomas, one of the "Anns," was expecting his kid, which was still another insult to me. I felt terrible that there were so many females in the room with me. Everyone, including myself, was aware that these women were Ike's girlfriends, but I felt helpless in the face of this fact. Even our strongest supporter and integral component of the Ike and Tina Turner machine, Rhonda, had to have an affair with Ike that she later came to deeply regret. Every single girl in our group fell for him. So, he went and did that. He equated sexual satisfaction with authority. When he conquered a lady, he felt like he belonged to her.

Sometimes his women, like Rhonda, ended up becoming my closest friends because we were all in the same position: totally reliant on Ike, always at his beck and call, subject to his rules and cruelty. As a group, we resembled cult members. Do they have a name? Sisterwives?

But I thought I was the one who was meant to get married! A notch or two above the rest? The reverse was true. When compared to his girlfriends, Ike treated me the worst. I was nothing more than a disposable vocalist, an object of use and disregard. My standing, self-assurance, and outlook on the world were all dwindling. Because I was becoming older and maybe more self-reflective, I began to entertain suicidal ideas. I informed my doctor that I was having problems dropping off at night. Possibly, I would have claimed that Ike was the one who need sedatives. He was an excellent doctor who cautioned me against taking too many medicines. I gave it the phony attention it deserved and then went home to stash them away for later use.

It just so happened that this was the night I finally had enough. I wasn't even thinking, much less considering the kids. It seemed obligatory on my part. Immediately after supper, I swallowed all fifty tablets, which is no easy feat. I anticipated their slow effectiveness and was prepared to wait for it. Even if I didn't perform, Ike would still be paid for the booking as long as I made it to the stage for our opening performance. That was the deal we struck. I had been warned that being ill before the concert meant losing all payment. Because of how well I was groomed, even my suicide had to work out for Ike. I made it to the Apartment, the club where we were playing, and began applying makeup in an effort to seem normal for the audience.

The Ikettes were in their customary pre-show frenzy of racing about and adjusting their costumes and wigs when someone finally realized that something was wrong with me. I had smudged my eyebrow pencil over my face and was having problems communicating. They panicked and scurried to Rhonda, who took one look at me and quickly summoned Ike.

I don't recall any of this, but Rhonda and Ike apparently forced me into their vehicle and drove me to the emergency room. Rhonda is the kind of person you want in charge during a dire situation. That night, she required her steely nerves and her lack of fear to get me to multiple hospitals until they finally located one with an emergency department. Rhonda was so scared that they were going to lose me that she constantly disregarded stop signs and ran red lights. While everything was going on, Ike was attempting to shake me awake in the rear. He was so desperate that he really forced me to puke up by sticking his finger down my mouth. Even though he would never acknowledge it to me, I can picture the thoughts running through his head as he thought about the money I brought in: Don't let her die, don't let her die.

The emergency department physicians at Daniel Freeman Hospital took control. The more they pumped my stomach, the less of a reaction I gave. I had not yet fully awakened. Inquiring, "Can I talk to her?" Ike posed. They had reached the stage of voluntary experimentation. He stepped closer to me, perhaps trying to seem like a caring spouse, and began talking. In my dreams, I heard his voice, a sound I was all too acquainted with: my tormentor's voice, a hell voice, cursing me quietly. Yes, he was able to go through. My pulse increased dramatically right away.

Keep talking," they urged. There is life in us.

The next thing I remember, I was awake in a hospital bed, attempting to recall what had transpired. The doctor or nurse entered and said, "Hello, can you tell me your name?"

A mumbled, "I'm Tina Turner,"

She enquired, "Oh, can you sing?"

When someone asked whether I could sing, I confidently proclaimed, "Yeah, I can sing," and proceeded to scream out the first line of "River Deep—Mountain High." It's interesting that I made the intentional choice not to sing one of Ike's songs even though I was only half awake.

A second nap ensued for me. The next morning, upon opening my eyes, I stared directly into Ike's eyes.

As he put it, "you motherfucker," you deserve to die.

I realized right away that I had not gotten away unscathed. My eyes widened and I told him, "Oh no." I quickly averted my gaze. Simply put, he was aware that the only reason I had taken the tablets was because of him. He just visited once and never came back. Ignored it completely. He was completely preoccupied with the performance. He had me go back to work as soon as I got out of the hospital. My strength was low, and I was experiencing excruciating stomach cramps, but I had to go up there and perform that night.

After we were done, the Ikettes helped me to my feet and escorted me to the locker room. The angry Ike was there.

Repeating, "you should die, motherfucker," he continued. "But if you die," he said, "you know what you would do to me."

It didn't make any sense to me that he would advise me to die, then tell me that my death would be horrible for him.

But back then, nothing made any sense at all. Ike was completely wrapped up in his own "I, me, mine." Everything revolved around him. Always.

Though I remained unwell for a while thereafter, I did get some insight from the ordeal. My suicide attempt wasn't a traditional plea for aid. When I took those drugs, I made the conscious decision to end my life. When I woke up, I felt miserable. However, after coming to a life-altering epiphany, I decided never to do it again. When I emerged from the shadows, I was certain that fate had ordained my survival. There must be a purpose for my being here.

In that moment, I realized that the only way out of this nightmare was via the door.

SOMETHING NEW WILL HAPPEN

A journalist once described my existence with Ike as "Dantesque." Having studied Dante, I now realize that he was not exaggerating when he said, "I went through Hell." In The Divine Comedy, Dante visits both Hades and Purgatory before arriving in Heaven. There's a lot of poetry sprinkled in, but ultimately it's a story about moving from suffering to calm, from ignorance to understanding. Ike sought to keep me captive in his shadowy realm of existence. For a while it was effective, but following my attempt at suicide, everything changed. My first seven years of marriage were spent trying to find out what I had gotten myself into, and my second seven years were spent trying to figure out how to get out.

Every day, I was subjected to a new layer of Hell. Ike, for instance, had zero tolerance for being sick. After yet another tour with the Rolling Stones in 1969, I became so ill that I could not keep my head above water. Unfortunately, the only automobile available was Ike's limo, and I had to drive myself to the hospital. In a conventional vehicle, I was a terrible driver, but in a limousine... I got it to my scheduled doctor's visit, and after taking one look at me, the doctor exclaimed, "You're going to the hospital right from here." So, I had to get back in the car and go to the emergency room. Finally, my TB diagnosis was confirmed. Not because I was unwell, of course, but because I was unable to work and our plans had to be postponed. The Rolling Stones were kind enough to send me flowers, but Ike was absent. It never occurred to him to come see me when I was in the hospital for weeks as I recuperated.

There will be more deterioration.

Ike had the bright notion to renovate the home while I was resting, and the results were awful. When we originally moved into the property on Olympiad Drive, the previous owners had equipped it with functional furnishings. There wasn't much to see, but the room was well decorated and cozy. Then, while I wasn't looking, Ike took control of the business and transformed it into a hipster whorehouse.

If you know me, you know that my environment is crucial to my well-being. My pals and I often speculate that in a past existence, I worked in the field of interior design. A home filled with candles, flowers, and timeless furnishings would be my ideal. If I have an idea for how I want a space to look, I can make it happen. When I was young, I lived at my cousin's home in Tennessee, in a rear room no larger than a closet. Even though the room was freezing in the winter and sweltering in the summer, I made an effort to make it more comfortable by adding a good bedding and artifacts I considered precious.

During our whole marriage, Ike never once allowed me voice my opinions. Once I moved on from him, I furnished and decorated lovely properties in England, Germany, France, and Switzerland. I consider my own style to be intrinsic to my identity. I had to accept Ike's choice in clothing since it reflected his own personality: that of a crude guy without refined aesthetic sensibilities.

What kind of furniture store would sell him that? And so, I pondered. The couches' unsightly metal spikes evoked unsettling images of phallic ornaments. The coffee table resembled a huge guitar, while the TV stand was designed to resemble either a whale or a giant snail. Everywhere you looked, bright splashes of crimson and gold could be seen. A mirror above the bed and drapes all around made the space seem like it belonged in Las Vegas. The kitchen floor was made of difficult-to-clean green-and-white tiles, and guess who had to spend half a day scrubbing it? Music producer Bob Krasnow stopped at my home one day and was taken aback to see me, the star of the Ike and Tina Turner Revue, on my knees cleaning the bathroom with a scarf wrapped over my head. What a downfall for Tina Turner's glitzy existence. Bob was not afraid to insult Ike with his sarcastic style of humor. He said of Ike's questionable decorating skills, "You mean you can actually spend seventy thousand dollars at Woolworth's?"

Ike was always upset whenever I attempted to make any changes to the home. I believe that he was so self-conscious about his preferences (a result of his limited education) that he became hostile against anybody who dared to question his judgment. If he discovered a change, he would virtually stomp me to the ground in his insistence that everything be restored to its original state. I went to change the bathroom towels once, and he really let loose on me. To paraphrase his exact words, "Get those fucking towels out of there and put back the ones that were here before," Tissues were the cause of this conflict. There was no leeway to act as one pleased. All I was to him was an object to be used and admired. During my tenure there, we never once referred to it as "home," instead just calling it "the house." True, but that was my sole real residence.

A successful outcome should have improved matters. We performed all around the United States, including at Madison Square Garden, and appeared on several television programs, including The Smothers Brothers Comedy Hour and The Andy Williams Show, because to the high demand for Ike and Tina's talents. The stage was no different for Ike in terms of his domineering and abusive behavior than it was at home. To this day, "I've Been Loving You Too Long" is my least favorite song because of how he had me perform it. The awkward hand movements I had to make at the microphone made me feel very self-conscious. Even anything as seemingly innocuous as turning my back on him during our performance would get me in trouble with him. In such case, he would tell me to "turn around, motherfucker." I was in a daze, operating on autopilot, and always worrying that Ike was watching me so I should just let loose and sing and dance.

When I earned my first standing ovation, I was completely flummoxed. In 1971, we visited Paris. The Parisian crowds went wild that night because of the excellent performance. They had all gotten to their feet and were cheering and shouting my name. The question was posed to Ike, "Can I go back onstage?" I had to be careful not to do anything that would make him angry enough to beat me up. I waited for his OK before proceeding. Even then, I was taken aback by the enthusiastic response and asked the crowd, "Do you mean it?" since I was not used to receiving such enthusiastic affirmation. It was encouraging to hear them shout "Yeah!" When I found out they loved me, I was ecstatic.

The triumph of "Proud Mary" in 1971 coincided with a general decline in quality of life. After hearing John Fogerty's song about Creedence Clearwater Revival, I proposed that we record our own cover of the tune. For a long, Ike and I experimented with it (as we often did with new material), but I had no idea whether or when we would perform it live. Those were internal choices that Ike made. Ike began playing the intro chords during our Oakland show one night. The tune seemed familiar, but I hadn't expected it. I had no idea whether I recalled the words, but I figured I could buy some time by chatting. I decided on the spot to improvise, "Every once in a while I think you might like to hear something from us that is nice and easy." The phrase "every now and then" was a staple in my vocabulary and remains so now. But there is one thing," I said. You have to understand that we never do anything simple or easy. It's usually wonderful and tough when we do it. Because we completed everything so quickly, what I said was somewhat accurate. While Ike kept playing, the tune's familiar opening lines resurfaced in my mind: "And we're rolling, rolling, rolling on a river." There was mass hysteria.

I was cocky as a rooster when I realized I could make the characters speak. Dancing being in my blood, I did what came naturally as Ike began playing the faster version: I did something, anything, to keep the onlookers entertained. I have no idea what I did wrong the first time. One of the Ikettes said after the performance, "Rolling on a river. So we came up with a dance to the lyrics, "Let's do what happens when you roll on a river," or something to that effect.

The group's "Proud Mary" also won the Grammy for Best R&B Vocal Performance by a Group and rose to number four on the mainstream charts. It was the type of widespread acclaim that Ike had always dreamed of, but it didn't come cheap. Ike was able to realize a long-held goal of his and utilize the profits from "Proud Mary" to construct his very own recording studio, which he now uses as his home base and which is just a five-minute drive away. He gave it the name "Bolic," a play on my maiden name "Bullock," to show his appreciation for all the help I gave him in getting his studio built. His action was really out of character. Most of the time, his mind just refused to believe that anything had originated with me.

Ike's demise may be directly attributed to Bolic Sound. Locks were installed on every door, and he installed security cameras so he could keep tabs on what was happening in every corner of the studio. Late at night, when Ike and his pals would hang around, nothing worthwhile ever occurred there. Ike would lock himself in the studio for five nights at a time, only emerging to eat and drink. On occasion, he would just pass out, at which point I would move his chair to the stairs, where his mistress at the time (one Ann or another) would assist me take him up the steps and into bed. Just then, he left. After three days of slumber, he would awaken slowly. His method of resting was consistent. After a day of showering, shaving, getting his hair and nails done (possibly by me), eating, and listening to the top radio station, he would get jealous of the other artists' work and return to the studio in an attempt to create his own hit. After then, the process would begin once again.

The Ike I knew when we first met would sometimes reappear after one of these binges. A common phrase from him is "I'm sorry, Ann." Unfortunately, the damage was already done, and all I could do was say, "Okay," and go on. It was obvious to me that his regret wouldn't last.

After Ike began using cocaine, things deteriorated rapidly. As if Ike Turner needed more time to focus on his sexual life, someone informed him the substance would give him more energy. Having sex was about all he did for a living. An interviewer once asked me a really frank question about my feelings about having sex with Ike. Can you believe it? her curiosity had led her to ask. I gave an honest response. Even if I did not like Ike's physical appearance, I had to admit that he was bestowed with some attractive features. What did it say about him as a lover? "What else can you do besides sex yourself up and down, or on the side?" I let her know. I yearned for adoration. What I really needed was a romantic partner. Just little politeness and consideration would have been OK with me. When Ike's sex sessions started or concluded with a beating, they became an expression of hatred, a kind of rape.

I still don't know what the deal was with Ike. Do medicines have such effect? And so, I pondered. That's a tough one to answer, seeing as how I've never used drugs before. Nothing has ever made me want to stuff anything up my nose. I saw Ike and his pals go completely crazy on the cocaine. The cocaine he used to feed his habit burned a hole in his nose, causing him continual discomfort that could only be dulled by more cocaine. Substance addiction becomes a never-ending cycle. In addition, he had a serious addiction to peach brandy. The two together proved fatal. The unpleasant, bitter dynamic between us only intensified with each inhale of his new drug of choice.

He burned me really badly by throwing hot coffee in my face. So many times did he use my nose as a punching bag that I could really detect the taste of blood in my throat while I sang. To put it simply, he shattered my jaw. Not having a black eye was something I had forgotten. To him, it was a show of might over me. The more he attempted to put me down and destroy my will, the more I had to keep my cool, seem like I didn't care about what he said, and generally act like I wasn't impacted by his treatment. Our closest friends and family members saw what was occurring, but they were unable to stop him. Rhonda, one of my closest friends (who also endured agony and humiliation at his hands, when he did things like yank her hair), knew him well enough to know that trying to aid me would only make him more aggressive. Ike's rapid spin out of control was terrifying.

Domestic violence was not a widespread problem in the 1970s. I spent a lot of time in the ER, but usually I'd simply pick myself up after a beating and perform anyway, bruises and all. I discovered that covering up my wounds with cosmetics, a bright grin, and some flamboyant dancing routines helped. The physicians apparently didn't think anything of my frequent visits and many "accidents," but they didn't say anything either. They undoubtedly assumed that marital strife among black couples was a common occurrence.

At one point, Ike referred me to a therapist. What an adventure Ike was. When I reflect on those younger days, I can't help but chuckle. He advised me to see a counselor. As you can see, I didn't hold back. I opened up to the therapist about all of our issues, including our singing, our home life, the challenges of being a single mother, and the fact that Ike wasn't a good parent. The therapist concluded the appointment by saying, "I think your husband is the one I need to see." After suggesting that Ike schedule a meeting, I returned to the studio. It never came to it.

I hoped he would stop bothering me and replace me with one of his lovers so I could finally go. In private however, Ike would refer to me as "my million dollars." It wasn't until much later that I realized what it meant. He needed my income to keep the lights on, therefore he never wanted me to go.

Ours was a blended family, in part because our marriage was centered around the musician's career. Ike regarded San Francisco, over 400 miles distant (and portions of Arizona, for that matter), to be within driving distance of Los Angeles, so we'd spend three months on the road and the next three months working six or seven days a week in areas within driving distance of L.A. We would come home for three months, then hit the road again. Duke's wife Birdie, one of Ike's mistresses, Ann Cain, and other "Anns" worked as housekeepers to take care of the boys while we were gone. My sister Alline was a doting aunt who kept a close eye on her nephews, and she lived nearby.

This was no ordinary family. I attempted to block out the thought that Ike's actions may have a negative impact on our kids. Because Ike was not the sort of guy who would worry about being a good parent, I had to take on the dual role of mother and father. He would often say things like, "I have neither chicken nor child; when I eat a hamburger, my family is full," as an offbeat way to convey that he did not have a family. He seldom left the studio and when he did, he was eager to dish out punishment to the youngsters.

I watched the Hendersons, the family I had worked for in Tennessee, and learned how to be a mother from them. They taught me what it is to be a parent and the value of instilling moral values in one's offspring. When the sons and I were together at home, we always ate dinner together and discussed the events of the day. We helped them with their assignments, and I watched them play sports. Having Rhonda around has been a huge relief for me in terms of child care. We'd all load into the vehicle, and she'd drive us to amusement parks and carnivals so they could have some fun.

My sons, now eleven to thirteen years old, were maturing, and sometimes they encountered difficulties associated with my Tina Turner persona. While they were wishing their mother was more like the other moms, I was performing as a raunchy R&B/rock 'n' roll singer and dancer. To make amends, I was a stickler about decorum at the dinner table. I forbade the boys from using profanity or slang and expected them to behave politely at all times.

Children will be children, despite parental efforts to keep them out of mischief. However, it was too slow for Ike's liking. The lads understood that if one of them misbehaved, he would punish them all rather than singling out the miscreant. That was exactly how he thought. As the boys became older, I feared that Ike's drug use, infidelity, and treatment of me would cause them emotional distress. Or that his risky, bad boy characteristics would be attractive to them in the manner that any adolescent would. They saw the posse, the parties, the expensive clothing and vehicles, and the seemingly endless supply of cash. I hoped kids wouldn't imitate Ike's drug use, criminal behavior, or authoritarian demeanor. The chances, though, were not in their favor.

Truth be told, I believe that Ike was a little jealous of Craig, his stepson. Craig was the model student, unlike his careless classmates Ike Jr., Michael, and Ronnie. He excelled academically, earned his diploma, and never broke the rules. Ike was envious of the little time I spent with Craig's dad, Raymond, but he would never acknowledge it.

I knew Ike was in pain without a shadow of a doubt. He seldom laughed, but when he did, we were all so relieved to see him smiling that we practically clapped. The rest of the time, he carried a cloud of worry with him. No matter how good life was for him, he was always unhappy. The best of everything was his: he was famous and wealthy, with a lovely family with a fur coat, a diamond watch, and the finest attire. But he never left the shadows; he was simply there.

Not only did he mistreat me, but others as well. All people, in Ike's eyes, were the enemy. Even at the airport, he would threaten to attack the ticket agent by climbing over the counter if she said something he didn't like. He had lost all sense of control and was being manipulated by forces beyond his comprehension.

Put aside the question of my happiness, the happiness of my children, and even Ike's happiness. His music was the primary victim of this misfortune. Ike was a dedicated worker and a gifted musician, but he was never promoted. He just couldn't seem to let go. He became mired in a rut, performing the same songs in the same manner over and over again. He would get into a rhythm and not break it for days, becoming so preoccupied with one song that it became incoherent. Three or four variations on the same theme and rhythm were typical of his performances. Nobody in his group had the guts to advise him to quit. They were all on cocaine and too inebriated to make sound decisions. Because of this, Ike never had any commercial success with his music. Ike was unable to adapt to the changing business environment.

On the other hand, I was stealthily striving to achieve that same goal. ..evolve. Two Tinas emerged in the wake of my failed suicide attempt. There was Ike's Tina, always knowing what to say and do. Onstage, I gave it my all. When Ike said I had to arrive at that hellhole of a studio at three in the morning to record a track, I sprang out of bed. I made him soup, massaged his feet, listened to his ravings, and took his punches. Seeing him waste our money on women, drugs, and anything else he wanted to indulge in was more painful than his physical violence.

The alternative Tina had developed impressive skills in suppressing her emotions. Whatever was going on with Ike, I did my best to maintain composure, objectivity, and distance. Although it may come as a surprise, I looked up to and respected Jacqueline Kennedy Onassis during these trying times for her ability to remain calm and collected under pressure.

When I first learned about the President and First Lady Kennedy in the 1960s, I was immediately impressed by them both. Because of them, I began to take an interest in politics. I studied Jackie like a hawk and was so inspired by her poise and style that I resolved to emulate her in my own life. Not precisely in her style, but my interpretation of it. I used to wear pearls often. When I went out and got a strand, people started commenting, "Oh, Tina Turner is wearing pearls." I'm not sure whether they were making fun of me or just really surprised. But why can't I just put on some pearls? I gave the style my own spin by wearing them with my own wardrobe, and I couldn't be happier with the results.

Beyond admiring her impeccable taste in clothing, I had a deeper respect for Jacqueline Kennedy Onassis. Her calm exterior belied deep feelings of anxiety, uncertainty, and exposure. According to what I've read, she has issues with her hands being too big. She fretted about her bank account. She had a hard time starting again after everything that she had been through. All of this resonated with me, and seeing her persevere gave me strength and encouragement.

I only got to meet her once, but I remember our encounter like it was yesterday. Ethel Kennedy invited us to Hyannis Port so we could meet her kids after a performance by the Ike and Tina Turner Revue, which took place possibly in the Boston region. We all went to the Kennedy estate and had a great time dancing and socializing there.

After that, I noticed Jackie and an elderly lady enter the hotel lobby from the restaurant where we had eaten while Ike and I were checking in. I got into a state of shock right away. I dropped my belongings and hurried over to her before I really realized what was happening. Usually, you wouldn't act like that with Ike. You remained close by his side, like a good puppy. However, I was unable to restrain myself this time.

The words "Uh. ..uh . ..I'm Tina Turner and I'd want to introduce myself to Mrs. Kennedy, uh, Mrs. Onassis.

Then she made a little motion with her hand, and of course I saw it and swiftly extended my hand as she glanced at me and murmured, "Oh, hello." in her recognizable little voice.

She said, "You were just in Hyannis Port with Ethel." The fact that she already knew a little bit about me made me happy, as it indicated that Ethel had told her about our time together.

Jackie was really kind, however the lady who was with her had a very bad attitude and kept staring at me to see if I would leave. When I first encountered Aristotle Onassis, I was about to remark, "If she's being nice to me," referring to Jackie, "then you, whoever you are, should be nice," but instead I greeted him with a cheerful "Oh hi, hello," as if I were already acquainted with him. Oh, I was a total wreck. To be honest, I felt somewhat inadequate in her presence.

I was still shaky from nerves when Ike and I walked to our room. I finally got to meet the one female role model I had ever had. I admired her zest for living, her resilience, and her calm demeanor. Because of her generosity that day, she earned my undying affection. Ike was aware of my feelings for Jackie and what she meant to me, but what did he say to me? I'm afraid the answer is no. Way too crude. It was sexual, as you could expect. That's how it was with Ike, and that's why I relished every opportunity to escape his company.

While it may seem foolish, one of my favorite ways to unwind and secretly enjoy myself was by driving my Jaguar. It was one of the few occasions when I was completely alone and unrestricted, and that's why I enjoyed it so much. Tina, I know what you're thinking: How did you manage to buy a Jaguar? Well, in 1970, when Sammy Davis Jr. and I performed together in Las Vegas, he got me my first Jaguar. He had a brilliant mind and a great creative genius, in my opinion. When we initially started working

together in the late '60s, he introduced us on his variety program with a rudimentary kind of a "rap."
Therefore, I don't want to spend time chit-chatting.
We'll skip the small talk and straight to the point.
We have a special surprise for you to enjoy right off the bat tonight.
And trust me, you won't be able to remain seated during this.
Simply because Ike and Tina Turner are performing.
There was a revue featuring Ike and Tina Turner. ..to you
Since our time spent in Sammy's company was so enjoyable, we decided to film an episode of his hit TV program The Name of the Game with him in Las Vegas back in 1970.
Some performers give flowers as a token of appreciation, but Sammy was the kind of guy who did everything on a grand scale. He quietly ushered Rhonda aside and told her he had a car surprise in store for me. I believe he recommended a Mercedes, but Rhonda (bless her heart) let him know that I preferred English automobiles. Presto! A beautiful white XJ6 Jaguar appeared out of nowhere and drove me to the hotel. Ike didn't mind that Sammy treated me like an equal since he understood that Sammy wasn't hitting on me.
Sammy's present reignited my love for racing vehicles. Ike bought me the new Jaguar XKE V12 roadster in 1973. The automobile was purchased by Rhonda, and I was the one to take it home. I'll never forget the feeling of driving away from the showroom for the first time. My life was so regimented that even the smallest opening of window or door was cause for celebration. When I was driving my

silver Jaguar down Wilshire Boulevard, it was late and cloudy. There may have been other cars on the road, but as far as I was concerned, I had the road to myself. The motor's vroom still rings in my ears, reminding me that it was ready to carry me anywhere I wanted to go (if I had somewhere to go). Even though I knew I would never be able to drive it at its full potential, I still felt the exhilaration typical of motorheads. After a long day at the studio, I always looked forward to getting in my Jaguar and driving home. Only five minutes away, but they were mine to spend as I pleased.

Paying more attention to spiritual and existential concerns helped me, too. Being a curious person, I've always had an interest in mediums and psychics. I think there's a greater mind out there, and it's my goal to connect with it so that I can see the bigger picture of life and its deeper meanings and patterns. A competent psychic may make my life seem like a movie that I can watch in fast forward to see how things turn out for me. Not that all they do is tell the future (though that was fun, too, particularly when it said I'd be wildly successful on my own). Psychics have also helped me get perspective on my decisions and behaviors.

When things were at their worst with Ike, I found solace in Buddhism. My younger son Ronnie was one of the folks who suggested I try it out. They told me that chanting may help me make positive changes in my life. My child told me that his peers had told him, "Mother, you can get anything you want." That was an unexpected turn of events. However, I hoped that this might be useful to me.

A buddy taught me a little more about Nichiren Shoshu Buddhism, and I began my practice gradually, chanting in secret at first since I was afraid Ike wouldn't approve. I've always been receptive to other forms of prayer since I was brought up reciting the Lord's Prayer. When I first started practicing Buddhism, I stuck with the Lord's Prayer and then did ten to fifteen minutes of the chant "Nam-myoho-renge-kyo." I didn't know what the words meant because the literature didn't really explain it, but as I fumbled through the little book on Buddhism my friend had given me, I learned not to worry so much about what I was saying. All I needed to know was that the music was penetrating somewhere deep inside me and altering my state of mind.

I found that through chanting, negative emotions were banished from my mind. My perspective shifted. The burdens of life lessened. My practice, as they say, was helping me retrain my brain, come into the light, and make the proper choices so that I could escape my dreadful marriage. The more I practiced, the better I got at it.

Someone once inquired as to the connection between chanting and singing. I tried to explain that chanting is not like singing a song, but rather the experience of generating noises from deep within one's heart and soul. There's music inside every everyone. I picked it up as I went along. When you're feeling depressed, you may uncover the hum inside yourself that can calm you. My grandma, Mama Georgie, only ever hummed, never sang. She used to hum quietly to herself as she rocked back and forth in a chair. Despite the lack of actual melody, I can now see that it was her method of connecting with an innermost part of herself. Her heart's song, so to speak. Everyone need to look for their own internal anthem.

I wish more people could see the value of spiritual practices like meditation and prayer. To be spiritual is to connect with your ultimate self, which is why the word "spiritual" often strikes fear in people's hearts. I was always spiritual, even when I switched from Baptist prayers to Buddhist meditations when I needed other language. My training has taught me to handle difficult circumstances with more composure and less emotional attachment.

I'm still just human, therefore I still get angry every once in a while. But whenever I feel down, chanting helps me feel better. Taking up Buddhism helped me see that it was up to me alone to make my life what I wanted it to be.

Ike's unfavorable reaction to my chanting dispelled any remaining concerns I had regarding Buddhism's efficacy. I had concealed my butsudan, a little cabinet containing candles, incense, water, fruit, and other ritual necessities, in a vacant room, but he found it. He said, "Get that motherfucker out of my house." Putting aside the profanity, I could see that the idea of a hidden and enigmatic existence on my part unnerved him. Buddhism, in his eyes, was just another sort of voodoo, and he didn't believe in or respect it. In general, he was terrified of things he couldn't fully comprehend. It felt good to exert some control over him for once. It was clear to me that he was the frightened one, worried that I would put a hex on him or something equally ludicrous.

The invitation to play the Acid Queen in Ken Russell's film adaptation of the Who's rock opera Tommy in 1974 made me think that maybe my chanting was having an effect after all. Because Ike kept me on such a tight leash, each time I was able to step out of his shadow was cause for celebration. As you may imagine, I was overjoyed. When I was younger, one of my goals was to become an actor. After returning from the theater, I would reenact the most tense parts for anyone would sit through them. The most fun I had was acting out gory deaths.

I thought my ticket to Hollywood was a flight to London, where they were shooting the film. Since I placed a premium on how I looked, I packed my own wardrobe in case I didn't get along with the costumes provided. God bless you! Imagine how they would have clothed me if they had their way. When I said, "Please. The Acid Queen's clunky platform shoes were designed by Russell's wife, Shirley, but I was allowed to use my own Yves Saint Laurent outfit and accessories. Ken Russell thought I was quite attractive. I recall him commenting that he didn't realize I had that much hair, but it was perfect for my role.

The whole time I was in London, I felt like a bird that had escaped from a cage, since it was one of the few excursions that Ike allowed me do alone (he was busy with something in L.A.). That there wasn't even a single guitar for Ike to play made me ecstatic; I thought to myself, "I can do this without you," though I wasn't permitted to say that out loud. Ike's confidence that I could succeed without him was gratifying; it was the second time this had happened to me (if you consider my work with Phil Spector on "River Deep—Mountain High").

It's hard to believe today, but at the time, I was completely unaware of the Acid Queen's ties to illegal substances. My wild and chaotic existence has come to an end. Despite that, I had no problem acting like a crazed woman in Tommy. That makes no sense. By this time, I had been singing professionally for sixteen years, and live performances are a lot like acting in that you have to put a lot of thought into your appearance, demeanor, and interpretation of the script, or in this instance, the song's lyrics. I had a great time filming and wished I could do more acting in the future.

As I was in London for Ann-Margret's Tommy performance, she offered me to be a guest on the Ann-Margret Olsson special. In 1973, while Ike and I were playing at the International Hotel and she was at the Tropicana, I had my first encounter with Ann-Margret. Rhonda and I managed to sneak away from Ike's watchful eye in order to see her perform, and we paid a post-show visit to her dressing area. Roger Smith, her husband, was taken aback when he opened the door and saw me. He told me, "You won't believe this, but Ann-Margret is a huge fan of yours and has all of your albums," and then he produced a stack of them for me to see.

After that night, we became fast friends, and we had a blast collaborating on skits and songs for the TV program. We even gave a rousing performance of "Nutbush City Limits," the smash song I'd written about my city. It was easy for me to put the lines "A church house, gin house" to music since they represent fond childhood memories. When the song became popular, I received royalties, which, given that I was still not being compensated at the time, seemed miraculous. Getting the cheque felt like a little bit more freedom.

I suppose Ike realized he was losing his grip on me when I started spending more and more time outside from the bubble. Through my chanting and my focus on tasks that did not include him, I was actively striving to separate myself from "Ike and Tina." Your lover would drop from your life like an autumn leaf, the psychic said all those years ago.

My isolation from Ike was gradually dissolving as new opportunities presented themselves. Something's going to shift.

In July of 1976, we took a major leap forward when we traveled into Dallas for a performance. Our earlier gigs in Dallas at Lovall's and Fort Worth's Skyliner had been huge successes, so we were looking forward to returning there. Unfortunately, Ike was still in the midst of a foul mood after coming off of one of his five-day cocaine binges, so the flight that day was anything but pleasant. During the journey, he insisted on sprawling out over me and Ann Thomas. Being around him when he was drunk was embarrassing because I could feel eyes on us.

With the landing, everything became more worse. It was a miserable ninety degrees outside, but Ike insisted on opening a melted chocolate bar in the vehicle. When he reached for me to offer me some, I backed away quickly since I was wearing a white Yves Saint Laurent suit. My unwillingness to share his chocolates with him apparently signaled that a fight was imminent.

At first, there were words. His every utterance was a foul language oath. This time, though, when he replied "Fuck you," I responded with the same phrase. It felt as though a long-suppressed part of my identity finally spoke out. Ike was taken aback by this and turned to one of his band members, saying, "Man, this woman never talked to me like that."

Then he began beating me and went to use his shoe as a weapon.

He was really taken aback by me. When he licked me, I licked him right back. Fighting the individual who had been so consistently unpleasant, disrespectful, and abusive felt great. There was a tipping point when I panicked, and it was the last drop that caused the bucket to overflow. To the Statler Hilton, we battled.

Blood had stained my once-beautiful suit by the time we checked into the hotel, and my face had swelled. When we got out of the vehicle, people stared, but Ike said it was because we had been in a "accident." I must have seemed like a devastated and speechless lady. Ike really want to think that he had, as in all his previous bouts, won the round. In reality, things were quite different.

In our bedroom, I pretended to be the same Tina I always was: a forgiving and empathetic spouse, worried about Ike's health and well-being despite his ongoing headache, bloody nose, weariness, and discomfort. I ordered him food, massaged his temples, and urged him to take a short sleep in preparation for our first concert that evening. He took in what he needed to, but all the while I was wondering, "What if I just grabbed a bag and ran?"

In any case, I did just that. I grabbed a little toiletry bag as soon as Ike went to sleep, wrapped a scarf over my aching head, and slung a cloak over my shoulders. Then I ran like hell from that place and that existence.

Even though I had forgotten it, I still knew how to get away from snakes.

A rush of adrenaline carried me down to the first level, where I darted past the hotel kitchen and out into an alley, where I hoped beyond hope not to run across any members of Ike's entourage. Since it was late and I was in an unknown area, I took refuge among the trash cans. The streets behind the hotel did not provide the ideal cover for a frightened evader. The buildings were small, and the surrounding areas were overgrown with weeds. What I think, do you? Those weeds, which reached my waist in some places, must have been swarming with creatures I couldn't see, but I'm certain my determination to survive made me oblivious to danger.

Fearing that Ike might awaken and grab me, as he had so many times before, I decided to keep going. For many streets, I kept going until I reached Interstate 30, where I saw a Ramada Inn on the other side. Overlooking the bustling highway was arguably the safest option, but I wasn't familiar with the region. When I looked around, the quickest way appeared to be to sprint down an embankment and over multiple lanes of moving traffic.

When I took that initial step, I realized it might be another one of my near-death experiences. The trucks' whooshing noises as they sped at me were terrifying, but the tremendous vibrations I felt all over my body as they passed were much more so. When an unsuspecting trucker saw a terrified lady racing by him on the freeway, he blared his horn. That's when I learned that a human foot isn't going to get you anywhere near as fast as a tractor-trailer. When I got to the center of the road, the vehicle was almost on top of me. I narrowly avoided being killed when one of the larger ones passed directly above.

It's no big deal for a rural girl to sprint across fields and engage in other acts of daring. But I felt like a greater force was guiding me that night. I managed to go over the highway and up the hill to the Ramada, but I soon realized that much larger challenges was in store for me. Ike's favorite threat was, "When you leave, you leave like you came," which meant with nothing. Actually, he was correct. My face was bloodied and bruised, and my clothing were dirty and soiled with blood, but I had 36 cents and a Mobil credit card in my pocket. Also, I happened to be of the black race. Where Dallas is located. I realized that any reasonable innkeeper would undoubtedly refuse me service under these conditions.

I went up to the front desk, presented myself, and told the manager that I was a woman who had just escaped from her abusive husband but was now destitute. But I promised to repay him if he gave me a place to sleep for the night. With my defenses down, I worried that this stranger might take advantage of me and maybe even rape me. I was exhausted and numb, so I didn't feel any fear or anxiety. The manager, fortunately, had a soft spot for me. I was whisked away to a suite, and he promised to bring up some hot soup and crackers as soon as he could.

I felt weak in the knees and on the verge of passing out when the realization of what I had done struck me after I closed the door. Hearing was really important to me at the time.

I felt both fear and anticipation.

It wasn't only that I wanted to get away from Ike. I was making a break for a new life.

WHEN YOUR HEARTACHES FINALLY END

I'd be lying if I said I didn't question my ability to find out how to live, how to support my kids, how to withstand Ike's fury, and how to go on the day following my escape. Even though I didn't know everything (or anything), life was wonderful after I got away from Ike. Leaving that horror meant the world to me, even though I was broke and had little hope for a better future for myself and my kids. It had been fourteen years since I had experienced actual independence. Naturally, I was anxious, but I couldn't wait to test my independence. I was 37 years old and beginning over.

As soon as I got back to Los Angeles, I had to get down to business. Kindly, Ike's accountant had booked me a flight from Dallas to Los Angeles. For the time being, I've left the kids at home with Ike. I use the word "kids," but in reality, they were in their early to mid teen years. Craig, my kid, had a girlfriend named Bernadette and was nearly as old as I was when he was born. While I was out of sight formulating a plan, I knew that my sister, my mother, and Ike's housekeeper would look after the boys.

For housing, I had to rely on friends, but I couldn't stay with anybody Ike knew, for fear that he'd track me down and attempt to compel me to return. After some consideration, I thought it would be OK to ask my Buddhist friends and their families for assistance. They were generous hosts, but I found their laid-back attitude off-putting. I hopped about for two months, squeezing into spare rooms and making do with whatever space was available.

Growing up in the Henderson household honed my attention to detail in the home. I have always been a perfectionist. The first thing I wanted to do when I moved into these, uh, "bohemian" digs was clean and clean some more. I did a thorough cleaning, closet organization, and garbage removal while my hosts were away at work or school. Tina's arrival guaranteed that everything would be spotless and ready for her inspection. This was how I made sense of the mayhem and proved my worth to the company. Although I was poor monetarily, I had a plenty of physical energy and was eager to put it to good use. It seemed to me that being someone else's maid was preferable than being Ike Turner's wife.

Cleaning was a type of rehabilitation, as was chanting. Buddhists have an optimistic view of the world and think everything is possible. It was crucial for me to surround myself with upbeat individuals during this trying period, so I sought out my chanting buddies for companionship. I had faith that they would boost my mood. "Nam-myoho-renge-kyo," I chanted, sometimes for hours at a time. After some time, chanting became natural to me, and I could feel its positive effects. A passageway opened up in my head and I was able to communicate with my unconscious self. Because of my training, my responses were calm and deliberate even if my natural responses are everything but. Chanting helped me keep my wits about me when I needed them the most. The hardest part was going to be convincing Ike that I was actually gone in a manner that wouldn't get me murdered.

Denial, anger, bargaining, sadness, and acceptance are the supposedly five phases of grieving. After waking up from his slumber in Dallas, Ike went through a roller coaster of emotions when he realized I wasn't there (and that there wouldn't be a concert that night, or for the foreseeable future). He probably thought I was being theatrical when I vanished after our huge argument. To satisfy his own ego, he convinced himself that Tina couldn't live without Ike. He shut himself up in the studio, sought solace in cocaine (and maybe a lover or two), and waited for me to come scuttling back. When asked by the lads whether they thought he would ever go back to locate another "Tina," he admitted that the thought had crossed his mind. So simple might my replacement in his eyes, he thought.

When I avoided him, he found me. One day, Ike turned up to my friend Anna Maria Shorter's home with a posse of stooges after discovering that I was sleeping there. When I dialed 911, the cops arrived and chased them off. His second approach was somewhat more polite; he asked a meeting. I agreed, but I had already decided that I didn't give a damn whether he beat me or attempted to murder me before we even started. I didn't care what he said or did; I was leaving.

I made it a point to provide an unflattering image. I went out of my way to be unattractive by applying too much makeup and donning an outfit that didn't suit me. Ike's Rolls rolled up. Duke drove us home that night, just as he had driven us to Tijuana when we ran away together. I went back there and talked sweetly to Ike, even though I didn't feel very polite. I avoided saying anything that may have led to an argument, so I was always polite to him.

We arrived at the restaurant in obvious discomfort. Ike looked awkward, like he wanted to say something but didn't know how to initiate conversation. I may have suggested that he say something like, "My life is ruined," or "I'll really try to do better if you come back," to show that he was serious about making up with me. But he didn't feel comfortable using those words, and even if he had, it wouldn't have mattered because I knew who he was and who he would always be.

After our conversation, Ike immediately attempted a new strategy. He loaded up the four young lads and sent them to me, along with just enough cash to cover the first month's rent on a property. To me, it seemed like he was challenging me to do it alone by making that motion. I hope to see you soon, pleading for a return to your former existence. The girl who enjoyed taking chances, I reminded myself. This was a huge step away from Ike's control, but after experiencing freedom for the first time, there was no way I was going back. A strategy was all I needed.

I knew I could contact Rhonda and she would be able to mend whatever was broken: the speaker, the vehicle, my life. Despite Ike's best efforts to drive a wedge between us, we've always had each other's backs. The past's petty jealousies didn't seem to matter at all. Some of the memories we shared were difficult, but now was the time to look forward. To that end, I approached her about taking on a managerial role.

I warned them that danger was knocking on the door. Rhonda knew exactly where I stood legally. Because of my departure from the Ike and Tina Turner Revue, we were forced to postpone all of our scheduled performances. Since I was the one who bowed out (Ike was ready and prepared to perform, but without me there would be no performance), the burned-out theaters have served me with subpoenas for financial damages. However, we were short on funds. Period. While Ike sat back in our nice home and old lifestyle, hoping I would fail, I had to figure out how to pay the creditors and sustain my family.

Rhonda sprung into action in her usual no-nonsense, get-it-done manner. Tina quickly learned that without Ike, no one was willing to take a risk on her. What they really meant was, "That's only half of the show," they informed her. There won't be an audience for it. It was quite challenging for us. The simplest employment to seek out was an appearance on a television program since we had no prospects (or a band, or backing vocalists, or costumes, for that matter). Using the alias "Shannon" to keep Ike in the dark, Rhonda approached programs like "Hollywood Squares," "The Brady Bunch," and "Donnie and Marie" in an effort to offer my skills. I'd receive a call from her saying that I was available on a certain day and that I'd be thrilled to appear on the program in question.

Thankfully, she was able to get an appearance on Cher's hit variety program. Cher and I may have startled each other when we first met in 1975, shortly after her divorce from Sonny. Unprepared for the sophisticated woman in a silk shirt, slacks, and high heels who never used salty language, she had expected the sensual "Tina" she'd seen onstage, the wild woman who was all legs, fringe, and shimmy. Meanwhile, I learned a lot about life from meeting Cher since I saw firsthand how content she was living alone. With Sonny gone, Cher was finally independent. I wanted nothing more than for her to have the autonomy over her professional and personal life that she enjoyed (her choice of music, her circle of friends, how she spent her time, etc.).

In retrospect, I can see that our circumstances were quite similar. When we first met, both of our spouses were much older than us. Cher and Sonny started dating when she was just 16 years old. We were never left to fend for ourselves, so we lacked the basic skills necessary to survive. We were A-list celebrities making a lot of money, yet we couldn't even split a bill amongst ourselves. In the 1960s and 1970s, many wives expected their husbands to handle financial matters, but we found ourselves in the peculiar situation of making all the money but having little say over our earnings.

Following the dissolution of our respective marriages, we inevitably found ourselves in dreadful financial positions that did not serve our best interests. Cher owed Sonny two million dollars to make up for lost earnings when she terminated their joint contracts. In my case, things were a bit different because of the cancellations caused by Hurricanes Ike and Tina. But Cher and I were both resolved to do whatever it took to become financially self-sufficient. While Cher claims that she performed at Caesar's Palace to pay off her obligation to Sonny, I worked at whatever job I could find, no matter how menial, until I was finally debt-free. Money wasn't as essential to me as freedom, as long as I was well and happy.

It was a blast to work with Cher. Onstage, we got along well. Whenever I was set to appear on the program, she would joke about preparing for "Hurricane Tina." Whenever Tina was coming over, Cher would often remark, "Oh no, I have to exercise because Tina's coming." When it came to dancing, she knew I was not one to flinch. I always gave it my best, and it was thrilling to see her strain to keep up with me. Our genuine fondness for one another shone through, and I believe the audience picked up on it.

It was a different tale when they appeared on Hollywood Squares. It was a game show where famous people sat in little boxes and answered questions in a tic-tac-toe style. The famous people would be asked questions, and the participants would have to say whether or not the celebrity's response was correct. I was pleased with my level of preparation when the producers walked into the dressing area to preview the issues we would be discussing. When the program began, the last thing I wanted to hear was presenter Peter Marshall ask, "Tina, where's Ike?" yet that's exactly what happened. It was a little unsettling for me. Then the inquiries, which I had not heard before, began. When we were on the air, I saw that the themes were somewhat different from what we'd spoken about, making it unlikely that you'd provide the right response. Even though I understood it was all a part of the game, the fact that I made a few mistakes nevertheless troubled me. My friends made fun of me nonstop throughout my Squares episode. They were laughing behind my back and said, "Mother's on a television show, making an ass of herself," but I heard every word. I attempted to explain myself, but they ignored me.

Never mind. To keep us afloat, I had to do many things that made me uncomfortable. I made an effort to keep my sense of humor at all times. Tina's Operation Oops was the name I gave to my early attempts at independent living since I made so many mistakes at that time. After a certain point, I stopped worrying about whether or not I was doing a good job. I finally accepted my inexperience and ignorance without shame. I may just say, "No, I don't know that," and resolve to improve my knowledge and abilities in the future. To stay alive was my primary objective.

I leased everything we needed to set up housekeeping in a beautiful bungalow on Sunset Crest in Laurel Canyon for my two sons. I was still quite concerned with their etiquette and would not tolerate the use of slang in the home. Still, I had more important things on my mind. I knew this was the perfect opportunity to instill in the boys the value of self-sufficiency and discourage them from becoming spoilt brats. They were accustomed to having maids and nannies, so it was an uphill struggle to get them to clean up after themselves, particularly on the road. They were resentful of their new situation, particularly since they could see Ike still living the same hedonistic life he had before. But I believe they benefited from the experience.

Our meager resources did not bring me down. Optimism is in my blood. When a couple decides to end their marriage, it's an opportunity to start over in whichever way they want. I appreciated the feeling of a clean slate that came with having nothing. Rhonda and I were experts at stretching a dollar from two coins. After an appearance would net me a small sum of money, Rhonda and I would go through the essentials that needed to be covered: rent, transportation, food (I enrolled in food stamps to assist with groceries), and legal fees. When the last payment was paid, there was around ten dollars left over, which we promptly divided. The original "Two Broke Girls," we had no shame in utilizing Blue Chip Stamps (the California equivalent of Green Stamps) to buy necessities for our home. Thankfully, Rhonda had a couple credit cards on hand for unexpected expenses, and trust me when I say that we made good use of them.

I wanted to end my marriage to Ike, so I filed for divorce rather fast. However, he wasted no time in procrastinating. He refused to accept that Ike and Tina would not reunite as a performing duo. I corrected him during a discussion with Mike Stewart. Mike oversaw our most recent record label, United Artists. Ike's representative inquired whether I was up for returning. Mike assured me that if I asked Ike for anything, I would get it.

No, Mike," I firmly said. Yes, I can relate. It's too risky for me to return to that setting. Once Ike starts using coke in the studio, he'll forget all about this encounter. I was afraid Ike would attack me from across the table. I had no idea what I was going to do or how I was going to pay my bills, but I wasn't going to let that stop me. There would be no further business or personal relationship between Ike Turner and his label. It was over now.

Ike was taken aback, for some reason. My denial stoked his anger and caused him to lose his cool. When he realized I was gone, he reacted violently since it was all he knew how to do. After learning of Rhonda's betrayal, he planned to get revenge on both of us. Worse worse, he had eager foot troops who would do his bidding. Ike was always surrounded by thugs who fancied themselves to be lawbreakers. It takes a really cowardly "gangster" to prey on two single ladies, four teens, and an elderly couple.

We were inside our house late one night when we heard a series of huge booms outside. When we checked, we noticed that bullets had blown out Rhonda's car's rear window. On another occasion, shots were fired directly into the home. Rhonda slept on the floor of the boys' room, and I hid in my closet because I was worried more gunfire would come through the skylight. Rhonda's buddy afterwards overheard Ike's thugs gloating about the incident. Then there was the time someone lit a fire next to Craig's girlfriend's parked vehicle in the driveway. To put fire out, we hastily gathered water and blankets.

Keeping my head on straight was crucial at that terrible period. To help me concentrate, I began chanting for four hours a day, two each in the morning and night. After hearing from a trustworthy source that Ike was discussing a solution to his Tina dilemma with another person, I took some, shall we say, "practical" measures to safeguard myself. He made plans with a hit guy to "take me to the ballpark," "football field," or any other idiomatic word for a killing field. That prompted me to contact a buddy for assistance in acquiring a firearm, and once I had one, I kept it on me at all times. Ike often sent individuals I didn't recognize to do his bidding, so I learned to be leery of strangers and always on edge about whether or not they were following me.

I got pulled over by the cops one day when I was out driving. Something in my automobile sparked their interest, and now they want to interview me. I parked the vehicle and walked to the curb as they instructed. When they inquired as to my whereabouts, I honestly told them that I was heading to a chanting gathering. When asked by the police, "Then why do you have a gun?" he appeared confused. The pistol had been protruding out of my handbag and had been the reason for my stop. Ike's purported salvation from the gun. I hadn't considered how obvious it would be or how risky it would be to drive a Jaguar while flaunting it.

It must have appeared quite odd to combine Buddhism with a gun. In an effort to justify myself, I began bringing up my husband, Ike Turner, and how I didn't feel comfortable since he was going to take me to the "ballpark." The officers at the station were familiar with Ike (it seemed like everyone did), but they cautioned me against breaking California law by driving with a firearm since my husband wanted me dead. Knowledge gained.

At several points, I felt completely alone. If you can believe it, Muh sided with Ike. Since he had the mansion and the Cadillac and the bankroll, in her thinking, he must be correct. She would undoubtedly say that he was the most talented of the bunch if you questioned her. She kept insisting, "You need him," as if she couldn't see that I was talented in my own right. To no avail, I attempted to convey to her the horrors of life with Ike and why I would never return. Despite my best efforts, Muh continued to show maternal tendencies for Ike. After being ignored by her for so long, it stung, but it wasn't unexpected.

However, I couldn't afford to dwell on the past. I was in need of income and was successful in persuading Mike Stewart to provide an advance so that I could underwrite a respectable performance. Rhonda booked us in cabaret settings at hotels and casinos, which attracted an older and tamer crowd than I was used to. Nonetheless, I was overjoyed to be back onstage with musicians and dancers, choosing my own material, costumes (thanks to renowned designer Bob Mackie, whom I met when I worked with Cher), and schedule. For the first time in my life, I felt completely free.

Every time I came up there, I attempted to remember that sensation of anticipation and anticipation. And the reality is that I always thought that the audience was entitled to the same magnificent presentation, with me at my utmost best, whether there were five people there or five hundred. I didn't mind that there were wardrobe malfunctions (we didn't call them that back then, but there was that night when I went one way and my "Big Spender" costume went the other way!) or that I was sued at every job because process servers would show up with their hands out as soon as they heard Tina Turner was on stage.

Being on the road was challenging, but so was returning home. I would hire a maid or have my mom and Alline bring them food when I was away to make sure the boys were taken care of. Craig, Ike Jr., Michael, and Ronnie were young men, yet I still refer to them as "boys" out of habit. When I got home one day when no one was expecting me, I found a cartoon representation of a bachelor pad. Unthinkable chaos! There was so much clutter, I could hardly make it up the stairs. The children moaned to one another, "Uh-oh, here's Mother," as I unexpectedly entered the room. They were old enough and wise enough to handle it, so I didn't try to stop them.

Once again, I returned after a trip to find my home deserted. Xmas has arrived. I was alone myself, and I had no idea where the lads went. Since I have always like spending time in front of a fire, my vacation consisted of lighting the fireplace and spending time in the living room.

Only one present, a vase from my legal business, made it under the tree. Since that was the only gift I received that year, I recall thinking the flowers inside were the most beautiful I had ever seen. However, everything worked out in the end. Every time I was put in a similar position, I learned to accept it. I stopped moping about and decided to make the most of being at home by reading and listening to music in the peace and quiet. My default state was one of joy.

The farther I got from Ike, the less I could bear to hear about the gloom in his otherwise bright world. He persisted in following me and would appear at inopportune times. He and two of his thugs showed up at the airport where I was leaving for a performance one night. Ike put up an intimidating front in front of my band and the young guy I had hired to be our guard; I always brought along a bodyguard because you never know what may happen on the road. Those playing instruments seemed to be saying to Ike, "Don't even think about causing trouble." I appreciated their enthusiasm for boarding the plane and heading to the office.

The guard didn't recognize Ike, so Ike just glared at him and asked, "Who the fuck are you?" I felt bad for the guard since it was never how I talked. A wild, foul-mouthed spouse was the last thing he expected to have to cope with as part of his job description. Ike then poured salt in the wound by calling him a "sausage ass." The guard had never heard such an insult before, despite the fact that he was rather overweight. Ike had no idea that the "sausage ass" had ties to the Los Angeles underworld. I had no idea such a thing existed until the following day, when a kind older gentleman called to ask if I needed "help" dealing with Ike after hearing about the airport incident. Apparently, they were trying to entice him with a trip to the "ballpark." I was so taken aback that I mumbled some thanks and gave Rhonda the phone.

It had the makings of a comedy, yet these events were very terrifying since they might have ended someone's life. We had no idea what Ike and his men were capable of, and there was no telling whether they were armed with firearms or knives. That's when I recognized something was really wrong with our scenario. Many marriages end without resorting to violence or hiring assassins. The divorce process needed to speed up.

Assets were being negotiated back and forth for what seemed like an eternity. Ike was sending me angry glances on the day we went to the judge's chamber to finalize the divorce. You're such a moron, I want to say. Is it really possible for your energy to reach me at this point? I am immune to your influence. "Young lady, what do you want?" the judge questioned. Ike snarled, "There's no jewelry." when I remarked that I'd left several pieces of jewelry at the studio.

I anticipated this outcome. Ike intended to use the divorce as a means of keeping us together. There was only one solution to prevent the endless fighting and escalating hostility that would have ensued. Forget the jewels," I pleaded with the court. Leave it everything behind. It's just money lost in blood. I have no desires. He questioned my conviction, saying, "Are you sure?" I responded that although I was confident, there was one thing I needed to ask. When we initially began performing as the Ike and Tina

Turner Revue, Ike trademarked the name "Tina Turner," and I wanted to keep using it. After the judge decided in my favor, all I had left was the name "Tina Turner" and two Jaguars—one from Sammy Davis Jr. and another from Ike.

It's hilarious to think back on now that we had two Jaguars but no money for food, rent, or utilities. I could read Ike's mind. *No, she's just too old. She won't take any action.* Repeated denials. Everything was blowing against me: being a woman, being of color, living in these times. And you already know my response to the question, "What do you do when the odds are against you?" I tell them, "You carry on. You can't seem to slow down. If you are slapped in the face, just brush it off and keep going. What about the pain you're in? You must not dwell on your current predicament or your prior mistreatment. You must press on nonetheless.

SUDDEN INFLUENCE

Thus, I acted accordingly. As I was walking, I didn't stop. There was never a time when I proclaimed, "Well, I don't have this and that." What I really said was, "I don't have this yet, but I'm going to get it." In my mind, I was directing my own life like a dance, planning out each move and, more significantly, determining when to take it.

When I was feeling a little overwhelmed, I recall thinking to myself, "I have to get management." It was 1979. Rhonda had me booked quite well on the cabaret circuit, but I had bigger ambitions. Aspiring to achieve the same level of popularity as the Rolling Stones and Rod Stewart, I hoped to sell out arenas and concert halls. That was a bold goal for a forty-year-old female vocalist who seemed to have seen her finest days long ago. But again, I never really gave age any consideration. My appearance belied my age. No one could tell whether I was really gray since I was covering it up with wigs. I continued to dance and even ran across the platform at one point. I had the vitality and vigor of a young man. I wanted expert advice to get my career on the proper path.

My dancer Rava Daly started raving about her friend Lee Kramer, who happened to be the manager of Olivia Newton-John. Rava insisted that I meet with Lee and his new partner, an Australian named Roger Davies, who had just relocated to the United States. I took her advice and scheduled a visit with them. Because of its success in Australia, my song "Nutbush City Limits" was well-known to Roger, and he was also well-versed in the story of Ike and Tina. He was just twenty-six years old, yet he came from an extensive musical family. Roger managed the renowned Australian band Sherbet during their heyday before relocating to the United States and working as a musician and roadie.

Roger and I still laugh about our awkward first encounter and how it set the tone for our friendship. Roger seemed to be in his early forties, which is a lot older than he really was. His office was crammed to the gills with books, documents, and everything else; it seemed like he was a hoarder.

How did I come across to him? Roger assumed I would seem much older than I did because of my background with Ike. The wig and the clothing made me seem much younger than my actual age. He listened to a sampler of my music, wasn't really taken with it, and glanced at me as if he weren't sure what to make of this peculiar paradox. Roger didn't say much, but when he did, it was meaningful. He asked me, "What do you want?" after some reflection.

There was no use in sugarcoating the truth, so I said it like it was. Since I had left Ike and was on my own, I had realized that I had ambition. Well, I said, I recently went through a divorce. The truth is that I owe money. I need the services of a manager. For my music, I need a record label. Data is required. Also, I want to attract sold-out crowds like those seen by the Rolling Stones and Rod Stewart. There, I laid out my whole plan. Roger may have thought my response was ridiculous, but he never said so. I instructed him to fly up to the Fairmont Hotel in San Francisco with Lee Kramer because I was performing in the Venetian Room.

When I left his office, I felt like I could face the future with confidence since I had taken action. I wasn't sure whether he'd really show up to the concert, even though he'd promised to do so, but at least I tried to make contact with him. It felt great to be making educated decisions about my job, putting myself in a position of power.

The Fairmont crowd in San Francisco was warm and friendly, albeit a touch stuffy. Fans of the Ike and Tina Turner Revue were not typical of the upscale nightclub audience who frequented the Venetian Room. They looked fantastic as they sat at tables, drinking drinks and watching the entertainment. My act, which was still developing at the time, needed to reflect the fact that I would be performing in a cabaret rather than the venues I had previously frequented with Ike. My outfits had a lot of flesh, glitter, and glamour, and they were a mix of vintage pieces and exquisite modern designs by Bob Mackie. I updated the playlist by combining current radio singles like "Disco Inferno" with timeless classics like "Proud Mary."

For two weeks, I continued scanning the throng for Roger and Lee, but to no avail. It wasn't until the penultimate night of the performance that they arrived in San Francisco. It meant a lot to me to have those two young men there, and just thinking about it makes me emotional. They showed up, and I thought, "Great!" Because I wasn't tied down, I knew I put up a terrific performance. At long last, I had the floor to myself. I conducted my own orchestra, and they played my compositions at whatever speed I desired. I was never motivated by financial gain. I did it because I enjoyed performing, and I think it came over to the audience. It gave them a boost. The women in their black gowns and pearls began to dance. One of the newspaper headlines in San Francisco has stuck with me forever. According to the sign, "Tina Turner Pulled Cobwebs Out of Nob Hill Last Night." It was accurate, too!

Roger and Lee made their way backstage following the performance. Lee was grateful, but Roger was really thrilled, which much gratified me since I could see he was the driven one. As two individuals on the cusp of exciting new beginnings, our paths were destined to cross. It was an artist that he was after. I aimed to get a managerial position. His ultimate goal was to construct a star, and I wanted him to have faith in me so that I could reach my own potential. Each of our needs was met. Roger reminds me of the brother I never had, and I like to think of myself as the sister he never had. As soon as we began working together, we became fast friends.

Rhonda saw my need for a boss who could think strategically. Even though Roger excelled at everything he attempted, it was his understanding of the significance of expanding his fan base in Europe that most struck me. Many Americans in the music industry just didn't care that anybody else in the world existed. Roger, maybe as a result of his background, was always considering the big picture. From Poland to Asia, he sent me on assignments. With his guidance, I ditched the glitzy Las Vegas/nightclub costumes and props and simplified my show. The dancers were slimmed down and the musicians were given black karate outfits. Musicians were not fans, but they were cheap and unremarkable. Our efforts to make the concert more rock 'n' roll were bearing the fruit I'd hoped for. I felt more joy than I had ever felt before in my life.

Finding a record label was the biggest hurdle. I'll never forget Roger calling me "Darling" and telling me, "Every door I walk through, I say 'Tina,' they say 'Ike'." American record executives were fed a steady diet of propaganda about Ike, who had a bad reputation for violence and unpredictability. Now I was tainted by his nasty actions. Roger persevered despite the unexpected difficulty of securing a record deal. Instead, it was his ability to think strategically that made him such a great manager. Getting a record deal was one of several possible goals, he knew. He was weighing my preferences and options to find the best fit. I believe my unwavering optimism always impressed him.

We'll be alright, I reassured Roger over and over again. At the time, Roger was also Olivia Newton-John's manager. The fact that he was able to successfully manage two artists with such contrasting styles speaks something about his abilities. At one point, he brought me a song he really like and insisted I put it on tape. I told him the truth (like I usually did) and said that I just couldn't hear myself singing the song. He gave Olivia the tune he had found. Her greatest commercial success came from the song "Physical," which was written just for her. My tune has to be floating around someplace. Simply, we needed to locate it.

It was in the East Village of New York City, in a club called the Ritz, when I had my own personal Cinderella moment. Roger insisted that I play at the Ritz, a beautiful old concert venue that draws true downtown music enthusiasts, so that I could establish a genuine rapport with them. On one of my two 1981 performances there, Rod Stewart was in attendance. After seeing me play his popular song "Hot Legs," he invited me to join him on Saturday Night Live, where he was scheduled to appear as a musical guest. He informed the NBC audience, "We've got a surprise for you," and introduced "someone who has been a great inspiration to me" (which caused one band member to joke, "Doris Day?"). Rod shot it down and invited me up on stage. Bringing the song to life was an incredible experience for all of us. I gave a hearty high-kick every time someone mentioned the term "legs." I got to showcase my "Hot Legs" routine to a whole new generation of SNL viewers who may not have been familiar with my work before. For me, it marked the start of some very wonderful moments.

The Rolling Stones invited me to open for them at a few of their North American shows after yet another night at the Ritz. My goal came true when I got to sing "Honky Tonk

Woman" with my band in the Brendan Byrne Arena in the New Jersey Meadowlands. What a throng! This was a far cry from the cozy cabarets where I usually perform.

In 1983, when I made my third performance at the Ritz, fate intervened in a manner I never could have predicted. With Roger, I was going through this. I begged him to spare me the "guess who's here tonight" announcements whenever there were famous people in the crowd. To me, everyone in the crowd was a special guest, and I was there to perform for them.

It seems like a lot went down before I even started singing that night.

David Bowie, a musician who hardly needs an introduction, was recently in New York City for a meeting with representatives from his record company, EMI/Capitol. David declined their invitation to go out and celebrate his new CD with them since he had other plans. He lied and said he was going to the Ritz to watch his favorite singer, who just so happened to be me.

David's suggestion caused a rout. Music industry leaders were calling Roger nonstop, pleading for last-minute tickets to the event. Capitol was really one of my record labels, but when I earned David's approval, I became much more appealing to Capitol. Not until much later did I learn any of this. The place was crowded and buzzing when I stepped out onto the stage. It was exactly the type of concert I love to perform in: full of enthusiasm, with an enthusiastic crowd cheering me on. I recognized some of the attendees, such as tennis legend John McEnroe and Hollywood actress Susan Sarandon.

David came to my dressing room before the concert with my old pal Keith Richards, and the three of them were giddy with anticipation. After singing David's "Putting Out Fire," a song he created for the film Cat People, I had a great sense of accomplishment. The fact that he came there to hear my band's version means a lot to me since I believe we did a decent job with it. We didn't want the night to finish since we were having such a good time chatting about music and drinking Jack Daniel's and champagne with the other two. The celebration was relocated to Keith's Plaza Hotel room. The best part of the evening for me was seeing Roger's expressions as events transpired. He was ecstatic. If he could have fainted from the excitement of being in the presence of his heroes, he probably would have.

With David on piano, Keith in fine form, and Ron Wood dropping by, we rocked out all night. We performed David's next album track, "I keep forgetting you don't love me no more," in which he sings the lyrics. Roger continued telephoning from the other room. He was phoning his buddies and exclaiming, "You'll never guess where I am! You'll never guess who's with me!" like a giddy little boy. Having everyone present meant the world to him. I had a fantastical rock and roll dream. We didn't leave until the wee hours of the morning, when we caught a cab and returned to the real world.

As it turned out, this was the new reality. To return to my Cinderella story, that evening at the Ritz was the equivalent of attending the ball (without the bit about Prince Charming) because of the profound effect it had on my life. Capitol Records was encouraged by the response they saw to my performance and wanted to offer me a recording contract. Negotiations between Capitol in the United States and EMI in England were quite complex, but Roger was like a warrior manager when it came to getting things done. at a twist of fate, we ended ourselves at Abbey Road Studios (after a fast, lucrative performance in Sweden) to record with Martyn Ware and Glenn Gregory of the groundbreaking pop-techno band Heaven 17. This middle-aged vocalist had a promising future in the eyes of Martyn, who was essentially a kid but incredibly brilliant.

The studio was where I assumed musicians would be when I arrived. Strangely, neither a person nor a musical instrument could be found. As in, "Where's the band?" Remembering Phil Spector's massive orchestra, I asked. Roger and Martyn described the new source of the Wall of Sound, which resembled a massive X-ray machine. Martyn used synthesizers in the creation of his songs. I didn't quite understand how it worked, but I was eager to try something different, even if it meant harmonizing with a robot. The catch was, I had no idea what to sing. Martyn had no time to compose new music, so we discussed our favorite songs and settled on covers of "1984" by David Bowie and "Let's Stay Together" by Al Green.

When I hear a song for the first time, I sing along until I feel like I really understand it, much as I did when I was a kid and listened to the radio. After a thorough understanding, I declare, "Okay, it's my song now, I own it," and proceed to the recording stage. I just get into the studio, grab the mike, and do it. When compared to other artists, I stand out. When I'm recording, I like to provide a complete performance of a song. As far as I'm concerned, it's a narrative that has to be told from beginning to conclusion.

When I was recording "Let's Stay Together," I had a serious infatuation on a girl back in the States. So that's why my cover sounds nothing like Al Green's. Al is the one who composed the tune and who appreciates music generally. However, my motivations were more emotional. Martyn declared victory as I sang the last note. It just took one try, and we succeeded. Sometimes I am referred to as a "one-take wonder." My version of the song, which was released first in England and then in the United States, was also blessed. Everyone loved it!

Being skeptical of success is inevitable after spending as much time as I did with Ike in the record industry. I was like, "Okay, fine," when they informed me I had a hit song. However, I did not realize upon opening my eyes that "Oh, I guess I'm a star... again." And of course, there was a catch. When I informed several of my female employees that I couldn't afford pay hikes, they resigned in protest. "The song just hit," I mumbled. The funds have not yet been received. My record label saw enough success with "Let's Stay Together" to green light Roger for a new album. And they needed it done immediately.

Roger and I went back to London, where I'd received encouragement and ideas from the beginning of my career forward, beginning with "River Deep—Mountain High." When the United States failed to support me, the people of England did. Nobody has once wondered, "Where is Ike?" They took me seriously as a single performer. When I was a youngster, my cousins and I would get together at Mama Georgie's home in Nutbush and put on impromptu performances, much like in the old Hollywood movies. It was like that when we first started working on the Private Dancer album. The song "Private Dancer" was really unfamiliar to us at first. One song, Holly Knight's "Better Be Good to Me," was played to begin. We only had two and a half weeks to record a complete album, so Roger raced around town in a little vehicle with a huge suitcase of tapes, looking for songs for me to sing. It was a humorous start to the undertaking.

After Roger played me the demo of "What's Love Got to Do with It," we had an instant and heated argument because I really detested the song. So, I'm wondering, "What am I going to do with it?" Dismissively, I said. I contended that it was not anything that rock stars like Rod Stewart or the Rolling Stones would sing. Roger was not in agreement. He took great satisfaction in his ability to recognize a hit, and he considered this song to be a massive success. Roger advised me to have an open mind and then drove me to the studio to meet the album's lyricist, Terry Britten, whom he had previously enlisted to produce two tracks. Terry was lounging on a seat, legs crossed, guitar in hand. He accepted my remark that he reminded me of a little child in good spirit.

Terry and I discussed the music, and he listened to my criticisms. He got what I was trying to express; I wasn't interested in doing something too frivolous or trendy. Then I realized I needed to treat him with dignity. I gave his words a musical interpretation of mine own, singing, "You must understand that the touch of your hand...," with weight and genuine feeling. Uh huh. Both the method and the result were radically different. What Roger was seeing in his mind, I heard in my words. The record got off to a fantastic start, and Terry Britten and I worked together successfully for many years.

At the time, Roger was also Olivia Newton-John's manager. The fact that he was able to successfully manage two artists with such contrasting styles speaks something about his abilities. At one point, he brought me a song he really like and insisted I put it on tape. I told him the truth (like I usually did) and said that I just couldn't hear myself singing the song. He gave Olivia the tune he had found. Her greatest commercial success came from the song "Physical," which was written just for her. My tune has to be floating around someplace. Simply, we needed to locate it.

It was in the East Village of New York City, in a club called the Ritz, when I had my own personal Cinderella moment. Roger insisted that I play at the Ritz, a beautiful old concert venue that draws true downtown music enthusiasts, so that I could establish a genuine rapport with them. On one of my two 1981 performances there, Rod Stewart was in attendance. After seeing me play his popular song "Hot Legs," he invited me to join him on Saturday Night Live, where he was scheduled to appear as a musical guest. He informed the NBC audience, "We've got a surprise for you," and introduced "someone who has been a great inspiration to me" (which caused one band member to joke, "Doris Day?"). Rod shot it down and invited me up on stage. Bringing the song to life was an incredible experience for all of us. I gave a hearty high-kick every time someone mentioned the term "legs." I got to showcase my "Hot Legs" routine to a whole new generation of SNL viewers who may not have been familiar with my work before. For me, it marked the start of some very wonderful moments.

The Rolling Stones invited me to open for them at a few of their North American shows after yet another night at the Ritz. My goal came true when I got to sing "Honky Tonk Woman" with my band in the Brendan Byrne Arena in the New Jersey Meadowlands. What a throng! This was a far cry from the cozy cabarets where I usually perform.

In 1983, when I made my third performance at the Ritz, fate intervened in a manner I never could have predicted. With Roger, I was going through this. I begged him to spare me the "guess who's here tonight" announcements whenever there were famous people in the crowd. To me, everyone in the crowd was a special guest, and I was there to perform for them.

It seems like a lot went down before I even started singing that night.

David Bowie, a musician who hardly needs an introduction, was recently in New York City for a meeting with representatives from his record company, EMI/Capitol. David declined their invitation to go out and celebrate his new CD with them since he had other plans. He lied and said he was going to the Ritz to watch his favorite singer, who just so happened to be me.

David's suggestion caused a rout. Music industry leaders were calling Roger nonstop, pleading for last-minute tickets to the event. Capitol was really one of my record labels, but when I earned David's approval, I became much more appealing to Capitol. Not until much later did I learn any of this. The place was crowded and buzzing when I stepped out onto the stage. It was exactly the type of concert I love to perform in: full of enthusiasm, with an enthusiastic crowd cheering me on. I recognized some of the attendees, such as tennis legend John McEnroe and Hollywood actress Susan Sarandon.

David came to my dressing room before the concert with my old pal Keith Richards, and the three of them were giddy with anticipation. After singing David's "Putting Out Fire," a song he created for the film Cat People, I had a great sense of accomplishment. The fact that he came there to hear my band's version means a lot to me since I believe we did a decent job with it. We didn't want the night to finish since we were having such a good time chatting about music and drinking Jack Daniel's and champagne with the other two. The celebration was relocated to Keith's Plaza Hotel room. The best part of the evening for me was seeing Roger's expressions as events transpired. He was ecstatic. If he could have fainted from the excitement of being in the presence of his heroes, he probably would have.

With David on piano, Keith in fine form, and Ron Wood dropping by, we rocked out all night. We performed David's next album track, "I keep forgetting you don't love me no more," in which he sings the lyrics. Roger continued telephoning from the other room. He was phoning his buddies and exclaiming, "You'll never guess where I am! You'll never guess who's with me!" like a giddy little boy. Having everyone present meant the world to him. I had a fantastical rock and roll dream. We didn't leave until the wee hours of the morning, when we caught a cab and returned to the real world.

As it turned out, this was the new reality. To return to my Cinderella story, that evening at the Ritz was the equivalent of attending the ball (without the bit about Prince Charming) because of the profound effect it had on my life. Capitol Records was encouraged by the response they saw to my performance and wanted to offer me a recording contract. Negotiations between Capitol in the United States and EMI in England were quite complex, but Roger was like a warrior manager when it came to getting things done. at a twist of fate, we ended ourselves at Abbey Road Studios (after a fast, lucrative performance in Sweden) to record with Martyn Ware and Glenn Gregory of the groundbreaking pop-techno band Heaven 17. This middle-aged vocalist had a promising future in the eyes of Martyn, who was essentially a kid but incredibly brilliant.

The studio was where I assumed musicians would be when I arrived. Strangely, neither a person nor a musical instrument could be found. As in, "Where's the band?" Remembering Phil Spector's massive orchestra, I asked. Roger and Martyn described the new source of the Wall of Sound, which resembled a massive X-ray machine. Martyn used synthesizers in the creation of his songs. I didn't quite understand how it worked, but I was eager to try something different, even if it meant harmonizing with a robot. The catch was, I had no idea what to sing. Martyn had no time to compose new music, so we discussed our favorite songs and settled on covers of "1984" by David Bowie and "Let's Stay Together" by Al Green.

When I hear a song for the first time, I sing along until I feel like I really understand it, much as I did when I was a kid and listened to the radio. After a thorough understanding, I declare, "Okay, it's my song now, I own it," and proceed to the recording stage. I just get into the studio, grab the mike, and do it. When compared to other artists, I stand out. When I'm recording, I like to provide a complete performance of a song. As far as I'm concerned, it's a narrative that has to be told from beginning to conclusion.

When I was recording "Let's Stay Together," I had a serious infatuation on a girl back in the States. So that's why my cover sounds nothing like Al Green's. Al is the one who composed the tune and who appreciates music generally. However, my motivations were more emotional. Martyn declared victory as I sang the last note. It just took one try, and we succeeded. Sometimes I am referred to as a "one-take wonder." My version of the song, which was released first in England and then in the United States, was also blessed. Everyone loved it!

Being skeptical of success is inevitable after spending as much time as I did with Ike in the record industry. I was like, "Okay, fine," when they informed me I had a hit song. However, I did not realize upon opening my eyes that "Oh, I guess I'm a star... again." And of course, there was a catch. When I informed several of my female employees that I couldn't afford pay hikes, they resigned in protest. "The song just hit," I mumbled. The funds have not yet been received. My record label saw enough success with "Let's Stay Together" to green light Roger for a new album. And they needed it done immediately.

Roger and I went back to London, where I'd received encouragement and ideas from the beginning of my career forward, beginning with "River Deep—Mountain High." When the United States failed to support me, the people of

England did. Nobody has once wondered, "Where is Ike?" They took me seriously as a single performer. When I was a youngster, my cousins and I would get together at Mama Georgie's home in Nutbush and put on impromptu performances, much like in the old Hollywood movies. It was like that when we first started working on the Private Dancer album. The song "Private Dancer" was really unfamiliar to us at first. One song, Holly Knight's "Better Be Good to Me," was played to begin. We only had two and a half weeks to record a complete album, so Roger raced around town in a little vehicle with a huge suitcase of tapes, looking for songs for me to sing. It was a humorous start to the undertaking.

After Roger played me the demo of "What's Love Got to Do with It," we had an instant and heated argument because I really detested the song. So, I'm wondering, "What am I going to do with it?" Dismissively, I said. I contended that it was not anything that rock stars like Rod Stewart or the Rolling Stones would sing. Roger was not in agreement. He took great satisfaction in his ability to recognize a hit, and he considered this song to be a massive success. Roger advised me to have an open mind and then drove me to the studio to meet the album's lyricist, Terry Britten, whom he had previously enlisted to produce two tracks. Terry was lounging on a seat, legs crossed, guitar in hand. He accepted my remark that he reminded me of a little child in good spirit.

Terry and I discussed the music, and he listened to my criticisms. He got what I was trying to express; I wasn't interested in doing something too frivolous or trendy. Then I realized I needed to treat him with dignity. I gave his words a musical interpretation of mine own, singing, "You must understand that the touch of your hand...," with weight and genuine feeling. Uh huh. Both the method and the result were radically different. What Roger was seeing in his mind, I heard in my words. The record got off to a fantastic start, and Terry Britten and I worked together successfully for many years.

I used to love seeing George instruct the other performers from behind the scenes. I was curious as to how things worked in the film industry. I believe he was taken aback by the fact that I wasn't a prima donna and that I worked well with others; he'd often tell me, "You are the most focused singer/actress I've ever seen." There was a part of me that wanted to scream, "You don't know where I came from! There can be no prima donnas here." Looking back, I can see that my performance in the film was less than stellar. But I tried my hardest, and that should count for something.

I liked Mel Gibson, or as I nicknamed him on set, "Melvin," since he reminded me of one of my kids. He's carefree and humorous in nature. It was a lot like working with a band when you're trying to get things done with him. After the movie ended, I felt horrible reading about his bad conduct since I had grown to care about him so much. Melvin took my remarks seriously, and he was grateful that I was supportive and worried about his well-being, so I gave him a photo of himself with the message, "Please don't mess this up."

I have an innate need to mother those I care about. This is just who I am. In an interview with Vanity Fair, Keith Richards aptly compared me to a "favorite aunt" or "fairy godmother" since I tried to look out for everyone in the band when we were on the road. Aside from offering VapoRub for sore throats, I would urge everybody who had a cold to wear a scarf and zip up their coat. My connections with others in the company have stood the test of time because I have a "Mother Earth" mentality while still having a strong Rock 'n' Roll streak.

The night of February 26, 1985, was the climax of the incredible journey that began with Private Dancer and ended with the 1984 Grammy Awards. Even if I hadn't been a bit off of it from the sickness, that night would have seemed surreal even in my finest condition. While performing "What's Love Got to Do with It," I went down a set of steps onto the stage and felt the enthusiastic welcome of the crowd. The music itself was great, but the backstory was much better. I believe I spoke with everyone who hopes for a second opportunity and works hard to make it a reality. Even though Roger was there that night, none of us foresaw "What's Love Got to Do with It" taking home Record of the Year and "Better Be Good to Me" taking home Best Female Rock Vocal Performance Grammys.

Eight million copies of Private Dancer were sold in its first year of release.

Don't worry, Roger; everything will work out.

Memories of the first high of my newfound accomplishment make me laugh now. Making Beyond Thunderdome, performing in individual concerts, and beginning the Private Dancer tour all at once meant that I seldom had a moment to rest and reflect on my life. I was so busy spending my unexpected windfall that I didn't have time to apply for a credit card. Truth be told, I'd always considered myself a shopping prodigy, but now I had the means to indulge. One of my goals for my "Tina Turner Comeback" interviews was to get an American Express Gold card, as I told People. I had to borrow credit cards from my boss and other people I knew before I was finally able to acquire my own. "Don't worry," I told the interviewer. As the saying goes, "I always pay them back."

I sang a duet with David Bowie about a month after the Grammys. When I remember it now, I get chills. After our night at the Ritz, David and I remained close. We became close, sharing a bond founded on deep appreciation for one another and same passions. He was a fellow Buddhist, just like me. He made light of the fact that he would eventually have to decide between a life as a Buddhist monk and a rock star. When I listened to him talk, I kept wondering, "David, how can you know so much?because he was knowledgeable about everything, not just music. He was well-versed in the realms of the arts and theology. He was a student of life, a true Renaissance man, and he would tell Tina with a chuckle, "Tina, I never stop studying." David always seems to me like a bright ray of sunshine. Quite literally, he was surrounded by a halo.

Everything there is to know about our relationship may be found in the music video we shot for his song "Tonight," which was recorded during a live concert at the NEC Arena in Birmingham, England in March 1985. My performance started with me singing, "Everything's gonna be all right, tonight," while dancing to the alluring reggae rhythm. Then David, dressed in a short white tuxedo jacket, emerged from the fog. The crowd was taken aback, and the building shook like an earthquake had occurred. He was angelic in his appearance. To express my astonishment, I almost said, "Wow!yet words escaped me. Instead of just standing there, I decided to make a theatrical double take. Seeing such a spectacle would make anybody feel that way.

I learned some interesting things about David during our dress rehearsal the night before. He had impressive acting and dancing skills. Though some vocalists may, others may not. The moment we had an on-stage hug was unforgettable. We gave off the impression of a blissfully infatuated pair. Despite the widespread belief to the contrary, and I apologize if I've let anybody down, our connection was never like that. In fact, we never even shared a bed. When compared to other rock stars, David stood out. A true gentleman, he was.

I guess I should move on to the next big thing. I'm not exaggerating when I say that "What did David Bowie whisper in your ear when you were dancing together in the 'Tonight' video?" is one of the most hotly contested mysteries in rock 'n' roll history.Reporters and fans alike want to know. Some have recommended bringing in a lip reader to assist comprehend what David is saying, but his mouth is so near to my ear that I can't make out his lips very well.

So, to recap: David gets close and says something, and I behave as though I've overheard something really inappropriate. He did not make any sexually suggestive remarks. That's something I'd keep in mind for sure. But I'm racking my brain for the words he really said to me.

The fact is that I just cannot recall. David is no longer alive to explain his comments, and we will never know what he said (though I doubt his recollection was much better than mine). Perhaps he has forgotten as well.

A young lady sprang onto the stage and grabbed David's arm at some point during our duet. David, who was hilarious and quick on his feet, made a remark along the lines of "I guess I should be glad it was a girl," meaning that the media would have made a bigger deal out of his sexuality if a man had done something similar. Even if people wouldn't say anything about his sexual orientation now, or may even characterize him as sexually "fluid," the fact that it was such a huge deal at the time amused him.

After we finished "Tonight," I said to David that I'd want him to compose a song for me that was in the same vein as "Putting Out Fire." He said he'd do it, but I had my doubts. Many creatives would enthusiastically agree to work with me at first, but then they'd become busy with other things in their life and forget about me. That's not David. A few months later, he contacted me while skiing to tell me he had a terrific song for me: "It's called 'Girls,' " he added, calling the tune "really rough," which was exactly how I loved my music. "And," he said, "if you don't take it, I'm going to do it."

I paused and whispered, "Hold on." If you feel strongly about something, it must be good.

When people attempt to create a song for me, they don't always succeed. You don't comprehend because I can connect to what you can relate to, I tell them. I'll accept it if they say they wrote it for themselves and would sing it. I thought "Girls" was a terrific song, a worldwide song, the moment David said he wanted to record it (which he did). I like the message that women are strong and mysterious.

When I was getting ready to record it, it took me a long to figure out what it was about, but that's one of the things I enjoy most about David's music: it makes me ponder.

David was performing in Brussels when I last saw him. After the show, I went to his dressing room to say hello and catch up. He kept his illness a secret from me, so I enjoyed our visit even though I didn't realize it was our "last dance," our last farewell.

A simple, "Love you, Tina" was all he needed to hear from her.

I replied, "Love you, David."

I'm relieved that those were the last words we exchanged.

When I first met Erwin, who has spent his whole adult life working in the music industry, he said, "Why did Bowie and Jagger take you under their wing? I told him that the English had been supportive of me from the beginning of my career with "Ike and Tina," and that they had become much more so when I parted ways with Ike.

They must have seen a lady who could hold her own vocally, work with them in a rock 'n' roll kind of style onstage, and make it all appear like a lot of fun. David used to say, "When you're dancing with Tina, she looks you in the eye." Equals. Nobody else could sing or dance like me; no other ladies could be seductive without being explicit. I went out in a short dress and heels and had a great time dancing and laughing without making any of the males there uncomfortable. Nothing unpleasant was ever spoken from center stage. Today, Beyoncé exudes the same vitality, but in the past, I was the only one who felt it.

There can only be so many ladies on stage with Mick Jagger. Despite this, Mick and I always had a great fun performing together; a prime example is our set at Live Aid in 1985, the landmark event organized by Bob Geldof to combat the famine in Ethiopia.

At JFK Stadium in Philadelphia, it was far into the night. The crowd had been there all day in 95 degree heat, taking in performances by artists as diverse as Tom Petty and Madonna, the Beach Boys, and Bob Dylan. They were now waiting for Mick, who would not be deterred by the sweltering conditions from delivering his customary energetic show. He had a very muscular personality (but I did like thinking back on his impromptu dancing lessons with me and the Ikettes in London). That's what they wanted to see from him, after all.

Before I surprised the audience that night to perform two songs with Mick, we had a little conversation regarding the pace. I was worried that Mick's support band, Hall & Oates, were playing too slowly because they weren't the Rolling Stones. I had to get going. It's too sluggish for me to dance. "Mick," I replied, "I don't know if this is going to work if they can't pick it up." He reassured me not to worry; he would handle it. He replied, "I know what you want." And with that, he walked out and arranged for the band to pick it up as soon as possible, telling them, "You want it fast."

His first question to me upon his return was, "So, what are we going to do?The two of us would never be able to just stand there and sing. This wasn't our doing. Taking action was necessary. I could see he was getting a dirty thought as he inspected my form-fitting black leather top and skirt.

"Can you remove that skirt?"subtly, he questioned.

"What!My stunned response was, "Wow.

That's right, "I'm going to take your skirt off."

It was too late to discuss it further when I finally asked him why. Mick had already decided to go through with it. "Just to create something," he said. Since this was the first time my skirt had been lifted onstage, I was understandably apprehensive. Lucky for me, I was ready. Back then, underwear was only the beginning. I donned dancer's briefs over my underwear and fishnet stockings over top of that to ensure that even if my skirt fell off, nothing would be seen save for another costume. That I was safe was not lost on Mick. True pros, we were.

Mick entered the stage, praised the crowd for persevering in the heat, and then yelled, "Where's Tina?I walked out and we launched into "State of Shock," which was nice but not thrilling enough for Mick. He took off his shirt and danced about shirtless as we began "It's Only Rock 'n' Roll," then he sashayed offstage to don a yellow jacket and camouflage trousers while crooning, "But I like it."

When he returned, his hand went straight for my waist. Oh my God, I felt him fiddling with the area around the snap. I had anticipated this outcome. I cast a quick peek below since I was curious about my appearance at the time. I was relieved to see that it wasn't that awful as he took my skirt off with a flourish. Everything was in its proper position, dancer-like, thanks to the support of the dancer's briefs, which served as a girdle, and the secrecy of the fishnet stockings, which disguised my underwear. Actress that I am, I feigned astonishment and hid behind Mick to give the impression that he had caught me by surprise. The reception was really positive from the crowd.

Mick is simply being mischievous. All we do is play. When I initially went on stage with him, he made a pass at my crotch with the microphone. He's just like every other terrible dude you had in school. For this reason, as the father of two kids, the Rolling Stones will always remind me of boys. Raising a kid means preparing him for a lifetime of fun. I never knew when the next of Mick's pranks would be, so I had to keep my guard up at all times. But he's like a sibling to me. It wasn't like some random guy just yanked down my skirt. That kid might have been anybody I knew. ..an elderly "boy."

Mick is quite witty. After I broke up with Ike, I went to see Mick in his dressing room after a show, and he joked, "I don't want any liberated women in here." He clearly wanted to express his joy and acknowledge the significant changes in my life, but he did so in his own unique way.

I saw Mick again at the Prince's Trust event at Wembley Arena in London, a full year after we had last seen each other at Live Aid. Due to his competitive nature, every conversation with him is like a round of Ping-Pong. My exact words were, "Oh Mick, your hair looks so good," to which Mick promptly replied, "Yes, and it's mine." He was pointing out the obvious contrast between my wig and his real hair. Nobody can out-argue him. Because of this, he always offers insightful interviews. In interviews, he always comes out on top since he understands how to joke around and redirect the reporter's queries.

Despite Mick's constant teasing, I can always count on him and the rest of the Stones to be there for me when I really need them. We're pals, I know it. To rely on each other is a given for me. Meanwhile, Mick and I will keep playing and tormenting each other for the rest of our lives. In this fashion, we do things.

When my career as a solo artist took off, I enjoyed the best days of my life. After the release of Private Dancer, I was in a position to take stock of my life and be grateful for everything that I had accomplished. I had toured with the Rolling Stones, Rod Stewart, Lionel Ritchie, and Bryan Adams; worked on the Mad Max film with Mel Gibson; won a Grammy; and recorded a duet with David Bowie.

Before I left Ike, I tidied up all of our trophies and plaques. I told myself, "Okay, I'm going to see what I can do on my own," and then I set about filling the blanks with fresh honors and certifications, as well as silver, platinum, and triple platinum record certifications. Of course, there is no such thing as a "overnight sensation," but there are second acts. The second time around, I didn't have to worry about letting anybody else's shadow cast over my own life, so I was free to make whatever changes I wanted. Ike has always made me feel like I was holding him back. But then I figured out the reverse was true. He was holding me back with every hit to my body and my pride. I could fly without Ike.

As Mark Knopfler put it in his song "Overnight Sensation" for me, "Overnight Sensation" says it all. At the time, we were in Canada. When he saw me play, he was inspired to create a song about a female who had "been out there a long time" after seeing me that night. Despite her time spent in the wastes, she never gave up hope. My initial reaction when Mark handed me the song was, "Do I want to sing this?" Do I want to be reminded of Ike and how terrible it was between us until I finally got away? Mark's song illuminated for me the need of my path, the fateful nature of my circumstances. Although Ike will always be remembered in my narrative, he was quickly becoming a vanishing sight. Future planning was more important than looking back.

Ike requested our boys to ask me whether I'd be interested in going on the road with him again when I began working with Roger. He even managed to strike up a conversation with Roger. If you can believe it, I think he really entertained the notion of going on a "exs tour" with Sonny and Cher. Roger, are you completely insane?" I asked. If we worked with Ike, you would not believe the chaos that ensued. The worst thing I can say about him is that he is a con artist. I couldn't even fathom sharing a stage with Ike, much less performing any of his songs.

For the most part, I avoided any potential conflicts with Ike. His silence deepened as the scale of my triumph increased. What a peculiar thing to happen! No more pleas were heard for a reunion after "What's Love Got to Do with It" became a chart-topping smash. I believe Ike has accepted the fact that I will not be returning.

After that, Ike Turner and I lost touch.

No communication right up to the time of his death on December 12, 2007.

AFFAIRS ABROAD

My lifelong ambition has been to perform before a sold-out crowd in a stadium or massive arena, like the Rolling Stones. I'm sure I've told poor Roger this so many times that he's grown tired of hearing it. The Private Dancer tour in 1985 made that possibility a reality. In only ten months, we completed 180 performances throughout the globe, from North America to Europe to Australia and Asia. In excess of two million people went to see the "new Tina," the solo singer best known for the hits "What's Love Got to Do with It," "Let's Stay Together," and "Private Dancer." However, I kept singing their old favorites like "Proud Mary" and "River Deep—Mountain High," and they were well received. Billboard magazine's description of me, "She comes to give," was spot on. Being on that platform was a dream come true for me. Can I ask you a question? "Are you ready for me?" I would poll the people around me. Holy cow, they were prepared! It was demanding, but I gave it my all from the moment I first stepped on stage until the last encore, which was often my cover of "Legs" by ZZ Top.

In connection with this topic, Billboard once referred to my legs as "the most kinetic legs in the business." The focus on my legs delighted me at the time, and it continues to do so now. Actually, I don't see what all the hoopla is about. Have you ever seen a newborn pony? Look at its legs! Thin and long? To me, that's how my legs have always seemed. I remember as a kid wondering, "Why do I look like a little pony?" I was born with a short torso and two little, hanging legs, but I've adjusted my wardrobe accordingly. No one in Nutbush would have given my legs a second thought. Black women with fuller figures were admired, but no one paid attention to me because of my tiny, straight physique. I'm not a very attractive lady, but I know how to make myself presentable.

After over a year on the road, I had very little time for my own life. I had gone a very long time without having a steady relationship. After my divorce, dating frequently became more of a hassle than it was worth, and I never had a lot of guys in my life to begin with (I spent my whole childhood with Ike). Never was I the kind of woman who had an unquenchable need to engage in sexual activity. To be really forthright, there have been periods of up to a year when I did not use it at all. Seeing myself on a man's arm would be significant. I didn't seek out male company for the sake of company. A couple flings here and there didn't amount to much. Don't make fun of me, but I've always been wary of becoming serious with a new guy because I'm afraid he won't like my wig.

Tina Turner's iconic outfit would not be complete without the wig. The audience wouldn't know who I was if I performed with my "natural" hair. People would ask, "Where is Tina?" When collecting my medical history, a doctor in St. Louis once questioned me directly about my racial background. I said "Black," and he started arguing. "Your hair," he said in astonishment, "is straight and lustrous." As is typical, he didn't notice I was sporting a new do.

When people mistake my wig for my own hair, it doesn't shock me since I see it as an extension of my identity. It's like my hair in a manner. Some performers treat their wigs like costumes and switch them out often during shows, but I never wanted that to be me. If my "hair" was naturally curly in real life, I would employ the same basic style and color while performing, but I would add more drama to the onstage version. I used to say, back when high hair was "in" in the '80s, "I prepare it like a three-course meal." I cleaned it, dried it, forked it, topped it with sticky stuff, forked it again, and dried it. The overstatement served its purpose, however. Onstage, I flipped it, ran my hands through it, and pushed it out of my face as if it were my own hair. Mick used to remark that no one could be sure that I wasn't really using my own hair because of the way I flung it about while dancing.

I see no reason to ever quit using wigs. As much as I appreciated the time savings and natural glow it provided, there was always the chance that a potential suitor may have qualms about becoming serious with Tina but then waking up with Anna Mae, bare of makeup and hair accessories. What if he saw the real me and was let down? Taking that opportunity has always made me apprehensive. The Private Dancer tour was keeping me so busy that I didn't have time to worry about this conundrum. At least, that's what I persuaded myself before flying into Cologne with Roger for a major event. The thought of the long day ahead had me feeling exhausted and discouraged. A young guy came out from behind a column as we were passing through the airport to say hello. Roger recognized him immediately and said, "Hello, Erwin." I had assumed he was a stranger or a fan. It was EMI executive Erwin Bach delivering the new Mercedes-Benz G-Wagon that Roger had ordered as a surprise for me. But the guy inside the automobile was the true shocker.

My heart, which this charming stranger apparently had in his palm, began to beat BOOM, BOOM, BOOM, drowning out all other noises. Coldness radiated from my hands. My whole being was trembling. I was amazed to learn that this was a case of "love at first sight." Oh my God, I am not ready for this, was all I could think, if I could think at all. The dreamboat in front of me extended his arms and smiled. I wanted to run into their arms, but I didn't believe in myself enough to do it. After exchanging pleasantries, we parted ways and left the terminal. As Erwin drove me to the hotel in the G-Wagon, I listened to him tell me the story as Roger got into our waiting limousine.

While we were driving, I glanced over at him and observed him. He seemed to be about thirty, and he was attractive in an unconventional manner. He had beautiful black hair and hands. The hands of a guy fascinate me. All of a sudden, I was really self-conscious about how I looked. Despite looking quite vibrant in my Issey Miyake sweater and leather trousers (very rock 'n' roll), I now realize that this was probably not my finest hour. Back then, my hair was huge and unruly. It was protruding because I had just forked and teased it, mimicking the typical three-course feast. That was my aesthetic; that was what my audience was used to from me. Even if Erwin did find me beautiful, I didn't think I looked very nice. Oh, as if the hair wasn't off-putting enough, I was also forty-six, divorced, and the mother of two—really four—"children" who, if I were being really honest, were virtually men.

Where did Erwin's thoughts take him? In retrospect, I see that he, too, felt an unexplainable electrical charge at the same time I did. My encounter with him was mystical, he said; he didn't see the "star," my skin tone, or anything else about me. He was captivated by a lady, a really attractive woman, but he was at a loss as to how to act on his attraction.

In the confines of the G-Wagon, our exchanges became more tense. There was a bit of a language barrier, and both he and I were having problems concentrating. Erwin was well educated and could speak English, but he hadn't been using it much recently, leading to some uncomfortable pauses. During the journey, which was somehow both too short and too lengthy, I urged myself to snap out of it. Speak! I was at a loss for conversation so I pretended to inquire where the fog light switch was and watched as he reddened as he fumbled about for it. We made it to the motel with some stuttering conversation about the dashboard and other unremarkable topics.

I hugged him farewell and staggered up the stairs to my room, where I collapsed into the bed while thinking, "God, he's wonderful." That's fantastic. When do I do what? Wow, I didn't expect that. I had no clue that Germany would be the place where I would experience true love at first sight. There was a strong possibility that we had met in a previous existence. I needed to find out how to make friends here.

I'm quite adept at what I call "knitting," or making things happen. The next evening, I had supper with the EMI staff, where I met Erwin. I decided on the spot to throw a Christmas party and invited everyone who was still in my life at the time. Then, in a flash of inspiration, I said, "Okay, everyone. I only wanted to get to know one person in particular, and that was Erwin. The more I learned about him (a psychic warned me that you can't tell him what to do, which is absolutely true to this day), the more I was drawn to him. The fact that he was younger and located in Europe was irrelevant. Let me tell you what I think. Maybe I just needed some love. I longed to feel affection for someone desperately. I could do anything I wanted since I was an independent woman. And I went with Erwin.

I was a bit of a bad boy when I was younger. I finally stated to myself, "I don't care" as we sat next to one other at yet another business dinner. I'm going to go ahead and ask him. He gently turned his head and stared at me as if he couldn't believe what he was hearing when I murmured, "Erwin, when you come to America, I want you to make love to me." He was so attractive in his Lacoste shirt, trousers, and loafers without socks. Even after I said it, I couldn't believe it! Later, he informed me he'd never heard anything like that from a female. Wow, he thought, those gals in California are crazy. However, I was no tame wild child. That was unlike anything I'd ever done before. I couldn't place myself in the room.

Erwin eventually made it to Los Angeles for business, and the group dined at Spago, Wolfgang Puck's trendy hot spot. After dinner (another of my not-so-subtle contrivances), I invited everyone back to my place, and that was the beginning of our passionate relationship. The music started, the other guests slowly left, and we kissed all the way to bed. That night, Erwin remained at my place.

Keep in mind that I came into this completely naive to the ways of love and romance. I was brokenhearted by my first love in high school. My first serious relationship was with Raymond, Craig's dad, while I was still a teenager. Then there was my wedding to Ike; you already know how that turned out. It took me a long time to start acting like a swooning teen, but once I did, I really enjoyed the emotional ups and downs of my second coming of age.

Erwin was flying off to Hawaii on a work trip the next morning. After dropping him off at his hotel, I went home, feeling on top of the world. Rhonda, the perpetual shutterbug, handed me some photos she had taken of us the night before at dinner, and I promptly framed them and hung them up. For the following two days, I kept thinking about Erwin. ..until he phoned and said, "Oh, by the way, we had to cancel our trip to Hawaii." He was in Malibu, not far away; he'd been there the entire time, chilling out with his coworkers on the beach, and hadn't told me. I put on a brave front, but I was seething with rage within. As I railed against myself, "Tina, you stupid old fool," I heard myself say. Why did I choose the wrong men? What was the deal with all the letdowns? The prospect of more pain was too much for me to endure. For my own good, I opted to do it alone.

Several months went by. When I was doing promotion for Private Dancer in Basel, Switzerland and bumped across Erwin, it was like old times again. For the holidays, I leased a home in Gstaad and asked Erwin and the rest of the EMI crew to spend time there with me. I was having a quiet evening by the fire with my friend Harriet when I longingly said, "Oh, I wish Erwin were here." His presence left such a profound impact on me that I couldn't help but think about him often. Although I hoped he would come to Gstaad with me, I didn't hold out much hope. Take cautious with your wishes, honey," Harriet warned. I don't know whether she was psychic or simply sensed something, but suddenly my security guard came up to say, "Tina, someone's here to see you," and when I opened the door, there was Erwin. I had received from the cosmos an answer to every prayer. What was I thinking? Happy. Excited. Nervous. Ready.

Erwin was sporting a weird yet adorable German country cap. I quickly recalled that I like every aspect of him, including the odd headgear. I couldn't help but be attracted to Erwin's machismo. A wonderful blend of boyish mischief and the calm maturity of an experienced hand. And now I knew he liked me since he was there on my porch. Our destinies were decided by the evening's conclusion. I've decided to move in with him while I'm away on vacation. My new permanent residence would be wherever Erwin happened to be.

Erwin wanted I do this one thing before we went public with our relationship. He treated his job at EMI with the utmost professionalism at all times. Erwin's father wanted him to have a secure, albeit unremarkable, career, so he urged him to take a job with a steel business once he finished college. Erwin had a dilemma since he saw a job posting at a record label that said, "Do you want to work with the Beatles?"Obviously he wanted to collaborate with the Beatles. He was passionate about music and eager to make a living doing what he loved. He answered an ad posted by EMI, was employed, and launched a career in the music industry, eventually becoming so successful that even his father conceded that his son had made the correct decision in opting for the Beatles over the family business of steel manufacturing.

Because of his position at EMI, Erwin felt it was inappropriate for him to date an EMI artist (me). To discuss the matter, he scheduled a meeting with Sir Wilfried Jung, EMI's managing director for Central Europe. Erwin was anxious since he didn't know how others would respond. What if he had to decide between me and keeping his job? He explained his predicament to Sir Wilfried, who listened carefully and showed signs of deep thought. At last, he opened his mouth to say something.

"There is a problem," Sir Wilfried said.

"Could you tell me more about the issue?Erwin politely inquired.

Sir Wilfried's comment, "I could become a little jealous," was code for "I bless you, Erwin."

One proviso, however. He warned Erwin, "Listen." That's fantastic if this is a true relationship. As soon as Erwin said, "But don't let me read in the paper next week that it's over," he was finally able to go on. This is how my romance started.

I need to pause for a second and address the obvious: our age gap of sixteen years. Neither then nor now has it ever crossed my thoughts as a problem. To begin, Erwin and I didn't start dating until we were both adults. Our age difference was far less of an issue than the inevitable differences in upbringing, life experiences, and personalities that plague all new couples. He's German and I'm American. That is the primary distinction.

For all intents and purposes, Erwin is Tina's "younger man," yet I'm sixteen years old and he's sixty. Erwin has always had the wisdom of a lifetime. He's much more grown up than I am. He plans ahead and is cautious, whereas I am more inclined to rush in without first checking my surroundings. He may be somewhat rigid in his thinking. As he did as a young child, he continues to enjoy playing his accordion. When we initially started dating, I was taken aback by his habit of shutting out lights and locking doors before retiring for the night. In response to my question, "Why are we doing that?He said matter-of-factly, "It's dark; we shut the doors and turn off the lights. I made fun of how much an elderly guy he sounded like.

The vast majority of individuals I told about my relationship were ecstatic for me. As a result of my actions, mature women were more comfortable dating younger guys. I was so sure that we would succeed that I ignored any criticism that was leveled at us. There's no reason for me to. I had already been through a lot in my life, including a horrible marriage. I decided it was time to prioritize my own needs.

My thoughts about Erwin mirror those I have towards becoming older in general. For me, there are no bounds. As long as I am healthy and up-to-date on the latest trends, I don't care if I am growing older. Humans are living longer, becoming more active, and even changing their fashion tastes as they enter a new phase of life that Deepak Chopra calls "old age." I have no interest in blending in with the teenage females. I've learned that I don't need to wear really short skirts or bare a lot of skin to look attractive. There's nothing wrong with me wearing more clothing to hide my age. All you can do is accept it and adopt a method that works for you. It is true that "You'll never get out of this world alive." That's not going to happen. Get on with it. You should put in your best effort in terms of your appearance. You must develop. I, like Erwin, don't see barriers based on age or skin color.

A few years ago, Cher and I had an interview with Oprah in which we brought up this same issue. Cher said about aging, "I think it sucks!" when asked how she felt about it.I had to disagree. I told the shocked crowd, "I welcome it with open arms," and went on to list all the reasons why getting older is great. I described how my life as a senior is superior to my youth in every manner imaginable: my knowledge, my style of thinking, my outlook. When you're still healthy and attractive, life takes a positive turn. When the number arrives, whether it's 80 or 90, I'll take it.

At the same time, I didn't appear any older than Erwin, who is thirty years my junior, when I was forty-six. When Oprah and I were alone, she asked whether I ever reflected on the fact that Erwin is younger than me. I declined her offer of help. It's like it's just Erwin and I here. Nothing requires me to make an effort to feel attractive in bed at night. Done with it. Exactly what role does love play here? A lot! We feel at ease with ourselves and, more importantly, with one another.

Therefore, I made the correct choice when, completely smitten, I decided to move in with Erwin in his flat in Marienburg, Germany, a posh neighborhood of Cologne that is reminiscent of Bel Air. I first assumed that the sparseness of his apartment was just a result of his recent relocation. After getting to know Erwin better, I realized that "minimalist" is almost his middle name since he despises possessions. I, on the other hand, like to decorate every available inch of space with books, candles, pictures, and scents. But Erwin believes that "less is more," thus his ideal coffee table would just have the TV remote on it. More on this to come. ..Erwin had a standard bachelor flat, complete with a terrific music system, in his two-room apartment. Erwin said that he had sold thousands of records before he moved and only retained a few hundred of his all-time favorites, yet there was art leaning against the walls and stacks of records everywhere else. At first glance, I thought, Wow, this place needs some serious decoration. I was silent and unsure of timing, but my mind was already racing with thoughts for the redesign.

My baggage was a bigger issue. In preparation for my month-long vacation, I filled around ten Louis Vuitton luggage with an assortment of clothes suitable for every scenario. Erwin's 100-square-meter flat was too small to accommodate all of that. My baggage were stashed in the basement, so I could quickly get dressed in the morning. Erwin's neighbors made their way around the pile of "Louis" every time they used the laundry facilities. Inconvenience aside, they couldn't believe their eyes when they strolled into the washing room and saw Tina Turner digging through her bags for an outfit.

On this journey, I was accompanied by my security team. Now that I was a "overnight sensation," I couldn't go anywhere without them, as strange as that may seem. While I remained with Erwin, the others went to a neighboring motel (where they could avoid keeping their luggage in the basement). It's not like I felt uneasy or anything. Having him around was a joy. When I was with Ike, I never felt like running away, but rather like I wanted to spend more time with him. I finally felt like I was in a real relationship. I reminded myself, "This is how it's supposed to be." We were two individuals who were content to live together and share a home.

After so many years in the music industry, I have no doubt that Erwin sometimes rolled his eyes at all the attention being paid to him. Be steady on your feet, he said. He gave me sound advice when he said, "Don't depend on the privileges that come with being famous because they can disappear as quickly as they came." But even he had to agree that having my security team around was a huge help. A walkie-talkie was our means of interaction. In addition to keeping me safe in public, they also made it so that we could spend quality time together in our own homes. When we were too tired to leave the apartment, they would bring us food so that we could eat in peace.

My excitement for our new life did get me into a situation reminiscent of an I Love Lucy episode once, I'll admit. My wildest plans haven't always paid out. Erwin had to take a little business trip to Brazil, so I remained put while he was away. As soon as he departed and I was left alone, the overwhelming need to redecorate overcame me. I didn't waste any time before rushing to Cologne's most well-known home furnishings store, Pesch. The standard lead time for ordering high-quality furniture is six months. I was advised by Erwin not to expect special treatment, yet the shop granted it when I asked for a next-day delivery. I moved my belongings about the flat in preparation for his big surprise.

Erwin's travel home from Brazil was ruined when a food cart ran over his foot, so he limped in on a Sunday in excruciating agony. The things he witnessed did not improve his mood. He felt as if he had somehow been transported to the wrong apartment, or maybe the wrong universe. There was stuff, more things, and more stuff wherever he looked. I had furnished and decorated the spaces. I even had an electrician come in and rewire his prized stereo for him. I was quite pleased with myself for getting everything done in only two days, but poor Erwin was appalled. He wanted things could revert to the way they were before I intervened. This was shaping up to be one of my most disastrous "Operation Oops!" moments."

Thankfully, Erwin had to control his annoyance since a friend was joining us for supper that evening. The following day, he seemed to have settled down a little and was beginning to adapt to the new circumstances. In the end, he decided to accept them. Isn't it amusing that he had more trouble settling in with the new couch than he did with his new girlfriend? We made it through that ordeal, but the struggle over decorations is still going strong. While I like to surround myself with antiques, paintings, souvenirs, and anything else I find attractive, Erwin still pines for that sparse space with a single table and remote control.

We eventually established our own schedule, if you can call traveling from continent to continent on a day off regular. Erwin was put to the test when I presented him to my family for the first time during the Christmas holiday, and he aced it. Even if Muh might be challenging, she appreciated that he treated her and Alline with such kindness and respect. Erwin was the inquisitive kind, while Muh and Alline were chatty. I wasn't shocked to see how well they got along. My mom and sister are so easy to please, even they can't say no to Erwin. He shared his admiration for their humility and found them appealing.

Erwin never directly asked me to be his girlfriend, but he sometimes inquired, "Are we together?" in his endearingly German manner. In other words, "Are we a couple?" I loved that even if it wasn't how we'd have phrased it in the

US. He was developing feelings for me, but he was nervous to take things further because of his impression of California women in general and my own cheeky advance toward him on our first date. He was afraid I was simply fooling around and would go without a trace. If he wanted my trust, he would have to earn it from me. To be honest, I was completely fearless. I didn't desire a spouse so much as I did love. Never felt loved as a child. Never really loved someone in the past. Never in my whole life have I felt true love. I needed to know that Erwin loved me more than anything.

We became experts at long-distance dating when I had to travel often for business. However, it was tough to be physically separated by an ocean for so long. It meant having to uproot often. I told Erwin that I needed a place to settle down. Since I still don't know enough German to live there permanently, I figured London would be a suitable stopping point before making the jump to Germany. Being in the city again would feel like coming home, and it would put me closer to Erwin. In 1988, with Rhonda's assistance, I left California for a new life in Kensington, close to Notting Hill.

When I initially moved to London, Erwin (who was still based in Germany) would fly over to visit on weekends. My home was a wonderful white town house, much like the ones I saw on my first trip to London in the '60s. I frequently reflected about my younger self, the girl who had longed to remain in the magical world of red double-decker buses, Big Ben, and "God Save the Queen." Here I was, twenty years later, finally realizing my ambition. I felt safe wandering the streets alone for the most part. The

English fans who did come up to me were always nice and respectful, so I was able to live a more private and unrestricted life than I had in other locations.

Consider Milan as an example. People waving cameras have followed me all the way to my hotel; after all, the term "paparazzi" was coined in Italy. I couldn't do anything else when I stepped out into the street without first stopping to sign autographs. I appreciated the Italians' passion, although it often complicated my ability to deal with routine tasks.

The amount of love and support I received from my followers everywhere I traveled in Europe was overwhelming. For this reason, Germany is among my top picks for a vacation destination. Even after leaving the Ike and Tina Revue and before Private Dancer was a smash hit, I never lost my audience there. In 1985, I performed in front of a tremendous audience of 12,000 enthusiastic and grateful fans at Olympiahalle in Munich, which was one of the highlights of my career.

For me, that evening will always be remembered as the first time Ike and I played Munich together. Unfortunately, only around a hundred people bothered to come out to the performance. Ike's disappointment and rage prevented him from performing on stage. I had to argue with him before he consented to let us perform, but I was successful in convincing him that whomever was out there deserved our finest performance. Nobody can understand the joy I felt when I returned to Munich on my own and saw the hundreds of people who came to visit me. A beautiful fireworks show capped off a fantastic evening with friends.

When I had to abruptly cancel a show in Sweden, the response from my devoted following moved me deeply. Unfortunately, I had a bad sinus illness and couldn't make it on stage that night. The promoter stepped out onto the stage to break the news, anticipating a hostile reception from the audience. Instead, the crowd showed its care for my well-being by applauding and cheering. They sent notes, sent flowers, and showed up in even greater numbers when we rescheduled. My fans are the nicest folks I've met on my travels.

For me, touring turned become a way of life. After the success of the Private Dancer tour, further tours included 1987's Break Every Rule, 1990's Foreign Affair, and 1993's What's Love Got to Do with It. I enjoyed how the concerts became bigger and better as the performers and crew used their creativity, talent, and resources to make them even more stunning. I also wanted to maintain it on a personal level. I aimed to provide the most satisfying "Tina" experience for my audience members.

During the first stages of the Break Every Rule tour, I did make a critical error. Although I sang it at the third and final concert, I left "Proud Mary" off the setlist for the first two. I felt that the audience may be getting bored of hearing it, and I was getting tired of singing it. When I reinstated it to the Amsterdam setlist, I discovered how much the band had missed playing it. The audience went wild and started singing along with us. I urged my coworkers, "We have to bring 'Mary' back." Even now, "She's still rolling on the river!" When we played "Proud Mary" live, the whole crew would stop what they were doing in the backstage area and join in on the fun, mimicking our every move (including the spins, hand movements, and head pops) from the song. As you can see, this is how we perform "Proud Mary."

I'm not sure how I chose the music that I did. It wasn't necessary that the music be one to which I could personally identify. Actually, I never cared for songs about my own life since I had already sang so many of them, and I eventually became bored of singing blues. I needed to have a connection to the words, but a catchy tune is what really gets me into the delivery. I like music that bridges generations and may be enjoyed by both young and elderly.

It's also essential to pay attention to the "set list," or the sequence in which the songs are performed. The first song I played in my shows was usually "Steamy Windows," a tune that was a touch wicked but also energetic and exciting, and was sure to get the crowd pumped up. A new set would begin after a few songs, maybe with a more somber tune like "Let's Stay Together." Song followed song until the last, explosive performance that included "Proud Mary" and "Nutbush," the songs that finally got me out among the throng. The musical composition was structured to evoke strong feelings in listeners.

The question, "What were you thinking just before you went up on stage? When did you usually do this? This is what went on behind the scenes. The act started for me when I entered my dressing room and started seeing myself as "Tina." Tina in her normal life wakes up, has breakfast, reads, goes shopping, and unwinds with friends. Of then, there's also the Tina who shines under the spotlight of a performance. It's like you have two distinct selves. They're comparable, but I yearned for more stage presence.

While I'm sure it helps certain performers, I've never done vocal exercises before a concert. However, I do recall that Mick vocalized and danced about a little bit before he went on. However, no one ever encouraged me to do that when I was first starting out as a vocalist, so my body never learned to function properly without one. We didn't have a phone in the house while I was growing up, and I think it helped me develop a powerful speaking voice. Instead of whispering, we screamed to our cousins across the street, so I had to learn to raise my voice to be heard.

Every time I started getting ready, I did it in my own dressing room. To begin, I would put on my makeup by sitting down in front of a mirror. I opted to do it on my own since I've found that professional painters can either make you appear too flawless or, if they're unskilled, like a clown. I was careful to apply just a little amount at a time. Even back in the "Ike and Tina" era, when I had to get dressed on the bus or in a storage room, I held firm to that belief. I preferred to tread lightly. Since the lips draw so much attention, I topped off the look with a bold red lip. Then I pinned my wig securely in place so it wouldn't blow off or get caught on anything.

When I went out with Ike, a reporter asked if she could spend the evening dressing as an Ikette. For the sake of her article, she decided to learn the dance steps, the songs, and the proper way to wear the wig, the dress, and the shoes before taking the stage. I don't believe she appreciated how hard we worked to get ready or how talented we were. We'd had white Ikettes before, so that wasn't the issue, and neither was her attitude (though by the time the concert started, my dancers were fed up with her). The greater problem was that she didn't have a single dancing bone in her body. About thirty seconds into the performance, her wig began to slide off her head, she tripped over her own feet, and she fell to the floor in an awkward Al Jolson posture right out of "Mammy." Ike's expression when she said that was priceless. The words that came next can never be repeated. After then, we lost track of her.

Nothing could have gone wrong with my outfit thanks to my meticulous planning. I was full with doubts and inquiries while I got dressed. So, how do I look? Do you like the hair? Do I have all I need to keep myself safe? I had to keep my breasts from flopping around and leaking. The bottom of my body then became a consideration. Was I adequately covered if my dress came up (or if Mick Jagger were to be around and pull off my skirt)?

I never gave any thought to how males might respond to my appearance onstage, and I certainly never tried to seem sexual. I made it a point to appeal to the ladies in the crowd, because if you can win over the ladies, you can win over the boys. I wanted the ladies to warm up to me, so I seemed to be having a good time rather than plotting to kidnap their husbands.

Most attractive outfits were really just sensible alternatives. Unlike the other variety, fishnet stockings were seldom on sale. I found that short dresses not only allowed me more freedom of movement while dancing, but also complemented my little frame. Neither sweat nor grime was visible on leather, and the fabric never creased. There goes the sexual allure.

After finishing my routine, I would take one more glance in the mirror. Tina Turner the performer, not the lady who entered the changing room, should have emerged if I had done my job properly. To put it simply, I was prepared.

On the way to the stage, I would always take my bodyguard's arm. You may call me superstitious, but I didn't want to ruin the event by injuring myself (by, say, twisting my foot) before it even began. There was always a lot of cheer backstage since we were all like a huge happy family. The band members were getting into the spirit by playing their instruments, dancing to the beat, and generally grooving. Once in a while when they were singing one of my favorite songs, I'd join in. I'd clap my dancers on the back and stroll on stage past them while they held hands and said a prayer. I didn't feel the need to do anything special before the performance since I meditated every day. For me, this was the quiet before the storm. I waited patiently in my assigned spot on the elevator. When the lights came up and the music started, I was ready to greet the crowd.

It's acting, but in a nice manner, if you know what I mean. You can't just be yourself on stage; you have to be someone famous. When I was on stage, I always tried to convey the meaning of the songs I was singing by acting out the lyrics and miming to them. I gave the people what they wanted, which was a theatrical performance. You don't know who they are or how involved they'll be at first, but you want to make a good impression on them anyhow. The band, the ladies, and I would have to collaborate if the crowd was unresponsive to our efforts to get them up and moving about. Whenever we were performing for "one of those audiences," I'd send the ladies a coded signal to indicate that we should put in more effort.

One day, I had to stop and introduce myself to the group. Oh, it's quite peaceful in here. I then began the performance. They quickly got to their feet and were fully engaged. Those in the crowd may be taking a "let's see" approach. They wonder whether the show is as good as they've heard. to bring them up to speed, you need just try a new tactic. However, in the end, we were able to convince them. I wouldn't have been satisfied with anything less than them having the time of their lives. Enjoying the audience as much as they enjoyed me was one of my greatest joys. When you're having fun, you dance in a unique way. I was inspired by them. If I waved my hand and they all waved back, I knew they were paying attention.

My dancers and I have a unique bond. I couldn't help but compare their beautiful looks to a beautiful arrangement of flowers on sometimes. And they were never meant to look pretty. On that stage, we put in a lot of effort, and our single action was planned. such that I could focus on singing, we choreographed our routine such that the dancers did most of the moving around onstage. They would come over and dance with me whenever I took a break from singing for an instrumental solo. The dancers made the motions appear natural, but they were really scripted. It got to the point where the females were so accustomed to following my example that when I collapsed in the midst of a song one night, they all did too. They assumed I had made up the dance on the fly, which was embarrassing.

Once again, I went tumbling to the ground after catching my foot on something. To cheer me up, I glanced to my saxophonist, but he simply continued playing. When I yelled, "Timmy!" he probably believed I was faking. Please assist me! My head dancer Clare shared my sentiments. She spotted me dead on, but assumed I understood what I was doing as I always do. I got up and resumed dancing even though they didn't offer any assistance.

I'm sure there are those who are surprised I didn't trip more regularly. They want to know, "How did you dance in those high, high heels?" Let's discuss those heels, shall we? After years of performing in front of an audience while wearing them, I finally found a system that worked for me. Always keep your weight slightly forward on the balls of your feet, and never remain completely still. The power of one's toes might shock you. I was dancing on a slightly slanted stage one night and felt myself gradually falling to the floor. My ten little toes rescued me; I couldn't believe how well they grabbed the floor in spite of my shoes.

I have a wall of shoes dedicated to my favorite shoe designers like Christian Louboutin and Manolo Blahnik because I adore wearing their creations onstage. But one of my hidden strengths was the master shoemaker Pasquale Fabrizio, who looked like Geppetto from Pinocchio. Cher introduced us. Despite being based in L.A., Pasquale's shop and employees, who sat on tiny stools at tiny tables, were reminiscent of European fairy tale cobblers. Everyone from Frank Sinatra to Liza Minnelli wore the outstanding shoes they crafted. Pasquale created a "last," or mold of the customer's foot, and utilized it to make custom shoes, fortifying the shoe's heel and sole with a metal shank to prevent breakage. Shoes that don't fit properly make it impossible to dance, but Pasquale's designs were so well made that they became an inseparable part of the wearer's foot and leg. My feet never bothered me while I stood, danced, or did anything else for extended periods of time.

On the night of my 1988 performance in Brazil's Maracan Stadium, my feet were crucial. Surprisingly, my Break Every Rule concert attracted over 180,000 attendees. In my wildest dreams, I had never envisaged an audience as large as the one that saw me break the Guinness World Record for the most concert tickets sold by a single act. It was too dark for me to make out faces in the throng, but I've been informed that there were more women than males present, and that they ranged in age from teenagers to their grandparents. They expressed overwhelming joy at being there. The difficulty of performing in front of such a large audience caught me by surprise. If I had asked, "How do you perform for such an enormous audience?" I would have gotten no answer from Mick. You feel as if you have to rush back and forth across the stage in an effort to reach everyone. I wore many miniskirts during the night, yet still managed to sweat off at least six pounds despite the record-breaking heat and humidity.

Later on, I learned that entertaining tens of thousands of people is really quite an art form. I figured out how to walk around the stage so that I could sing to each section of the stadium without ever having to face the same section again. I switched between sections of the audience during the performance, tailoring the spectacle to each individual.

Therefore, I began making use of displays. I'm aware that some performers find them distracting since they prefer a more "real" concert setting. But how can you move a crowd in a huge stadium when some of the spectators may be more than a mile distant from the stage? Those faraway folks are always on my mind. For my performance to have the same impact on them as it does on the audience in the front rows, it is crucial that they be able to see every nuance of my choreography and every emotion on my face when I sing.

The thought of having a stadium packed with people who came only to watch me perform was always a pipe dream of mine. Wow, have things taken a great turn in my life. When I thought I'd never find happiness again, when I thought love wouldn't be a part of my tale, I suddenly found myself surrounded by it. After the release of my autobiography, I, Tina, in 1986 (and the subsequent film adaptation, What's Love Got to Do with It, in 1993), I was inundated with love, support, and gratitude from women and men who heard my story and were inspired by it. I also enjoyed the warm embrace of my audience at every concert.

I was really taken aback by that. For obvious and sometimes less apparent reasons, I avoided discussing my time spent with Ike for a long time. When folks found out the terrible facts, I was mortified. Even though I sought to avoid it, I now find myself imprisoned in a drab existence. Then I was obligated to speak about it endlessly. When others found out what had transpired between us, I was at a loss for words. They felt quite individual. What kept you here? Exactly what prompted your departure? I don't understand why you kept quiet at the moment. What are your scars like? How could I ever make anybody else understand if I couldn't even explain it to myself? I finally managed to put all that agony and perplexity behind me, but it took decades.

I just couldn't bring myself to watch What's Love Got to Do with It because of how sad I felt the subject matter. Some of the decisions made by the filmmakers, such as the way we were dressed (which was quite "zoot suit," meaning excessive and even disgusting), left a bad taste in my mouth when I saw a few segments on television. Even though they shot at our real home, they still managed to get the house incorrect. They made us look like we were from another planet. Despite our shared commitment to the creative process, I was not interested in spending two hours revisiting a nightmare I had spent years trying to put behind me.

As much as I wanted to forget about Ike and our history, I was touched to learn that my tragedy might inspire others. Many times during our interviews, Oprah would ask me the same difficult question: "Do you remember the first time Ike hit you?" She sensed my exhaustion and replied quietly, "Tina, you know why I keep asking." Oprah found more meaning in what we were talking about. She enlightened me to the fact that I was imparting knowledge by maintaining my line of discourse. It was a chance to open a line of communication with battered women and call attention to a taboo problem. Maybe if I told them the truth about what happened to me, they would have the strength to change their own circumstances.

Countless people have informed me that my story—my escape from Ike, my drive to live on my own, my commitment, my tenacity, and yes, my optimism—has helped them in some way, either directly or indirectly. Every time Roger and I went through an airport on tour, someone would approach us to tell us a tale. A guy yelled at me, "Tina Turner—I saw your movie and I will never beat my wife again," which was a horrible but ultimately wonderful message.

A lady who was abused by her partner told Oprah, "I came because I was looking for the courage to leave the man who beats me." Oprah and the woman sat next to one other during one of my Wildest Dreams performances. I finally mustered up the nerve to do it tonight. "You don't just dance and sing," Oprah said to me. You are the embodiment of hope. People will know you've conquered your demons when they see your performance. Whatever a woman's circumstances, she has the potential to be just like you.

I was once said to be David Bowie's "phoenix rising from the ashes." I realize how cheesy it sounds now, but when he said it, it was poetry, and his words perfectly captured how I felt. I want everyone in an abusive relationship to know that it doesn't get much worse than this. There are new opportunities waiting for you on the other side of getting up and leaving. But you must follow your own path. I've done the best I could with what I knew at the time, and I think that's paid off. I never expected my life to have any kind of significance, but I'm glad it may serve as an example to others.

ABSOLUTE MASTERY

One of my favorite photos was taken by the legendary photographer Peter Lindbergh in Paris during the shoot for the cover of my album Foreign Affair in 1989. Peter had me go closer to the edge of the Eiffel Tower for a photo op and we were there. That's not good enough, I told myself. Remember, I was the kid who was always up in the trees. Despite this, I still enjoyed thrilling people with my photographs and revisiting my earlier preference for risk. Rather than just looking at the Eiffel Tower, why not scale it?

I was wearing a dress by my late friend and designer Azzedine Alaia. The minute you put on one of his outfits, you feel and look extremely French. I believe I made Peter apprehensive when I suggested doing something a little extreme; he glanced down at my high heels and said, "With the shoes?" Roger, meantime, was about to collapse from a heart attack. "Don't do it in case you fall, the insurance will never cover it," he attempted to spit out as fast as he could to try to dissuade me. But I paid him no mind and climbed the wall nonetheless. With the beautiful City of Lights as a backdrop, I shifted my weight onto my heels, grabbed on with one arm, tossed my hair, and straightened my back. I envisioned myself doing just that, with all of Europe at my fingertips. My comfort level in the Old World grew with each passing year, and I eventually settled on making it my permanent home.

I was really contemplating making Europe my permanent home for a variety of reasons. One reason I felt secure away from home was because there was zero likelihood of my stumbling across Ike or seeing any reminders of our shared past. Someone gave me a program to sign at my 1991 Rock and Roll Hall of Fame induction ceremony in New York's Waldorf Astoria, and to my surprise, I saw Ike's signature there as well. We didn't really meet that day (or ever again, for that matter), but our close call made me appreciate the fact that I wasn't always on edge about running into him. In a new nation, I could easily put him out of my mind.

As my career progressed, I also felt that I was having the most success in other countries. In the United States, the focus was on having a number one album. Some music was banned because its creators thought it was too black to be white or too white to be black. Discrimination seems to be lower in Europe. There was a rapid increase in my fan base, my supporters were really devoted, and many talented musicians, songwriters, and producers were eager to collaborate with me.

The biggest motivation to relocate to Europe, though, was falling in love with a lovely guy from that continent. So that Erwin and I could settle down together, it seemed logical for me to go to Germany. Because of Erwin, Cologne quickly became like a second home for me. In 1990, my family and I discovered a beautiful brick home and spent months restoring it. I fell in love with a property in the South of France as well, since living in even one stunning European metropolis isn't enough. I live in the mountains above Nice, where a clairvoyant said I would have a home surrounded by flowers. I chose the name "Anna Fleur" to pay tribute to my given name, Anna, and the flowers. This traditional mansion was the pinnacle of my enthusiasm for interior design. I mixed antiques from the Louis XVI era with Art Deco and modern French furniture and anything else caught my eye, and it all came together beautifully, just as I had imagined it would. Every morning, I start in the room I've set aside for meditation on the second level. Over the course of many years, I transformed my home into the safe haven of my dreams.

Mike Wallace of 60 Minutes visited me at "Anna Fleur" for an interview. We had a wonderful day just hanging around and chatting openly while exploring the home and grounds. When he took a good look around, he finally asked me whether I was certain I deserved all this comfort. Without hesitation, I said, "I deserve more." I'd been in the workforce for close to four decades, and I'd worked hard for every penny. I felt grateful and proud of myself whenever I had the emotional gratification of being with the guy I loved or the material richness that came with professional achievement. I was deserving of it, too.

Bono and The Edge of U2 both have residences in Eze-sur-Mer, a little village not far from Nice, where I was staying. I was asked over for supper one night, and as I was making my way up the driveway, I heard a person remark on my voice, and I knew immediately that it was Jack Nicholson's drawling, "I hear you coming." We both appeared in Tommy, but we never worked together on the film, so this was our first opportunity to meet. All night long we spoke and shared anecdotes about our time in the spotlight as singers and actors. When they were composing the theme song for the upcoming James Bond movie, GoldenEye, Bono and The Edge said that they wanted me to sing it.

I was ecstatic... until I heard Bono's demo, which consisted of disjointed musical fragments that failed to form a coherent whole. A question: what is this? So, I pondered. What key should I be singing it in? I had no idea. Bono added that after sending it, he realized how terrible it was, so there was something to make light of. But I urged myself to put myself in the situation and figure it out. I internalized it and performed it in my own style, and everyone, even Bono, loved it. We may have done a few takes to get it right. After that, I came to like the way "GoldenEye" altered my voice. I had never attempted a song like that before, and the challenge of converting those raw bits into a polished, emotionally expressive song that served the film well and became a concert highlight was a welcome one.

The music video for "GoldenEye" radiated glitz and beauty. My hair was done in an imitation chignon. I donned a white evening dress that fit snugly off the shoulders and had a high slit that showed off my legs beautifully with every step. And to round it off, I put on a pair of lengthy, diamond-studded earrings. I thought the music was perfect with this startling visual, which was a brilliant mashup of Shirley Bassey's "Goldfinger" from the '70s and modern-day Bond.

While I was satisfied in each of the several locations that Erwin and I called home throughout our first decade together, I found a whole new level of happiness when we finally settled in Switzerland in 1995. I use the word "destiny," but the reality is far less romantic. Erwin was asked to head up EMI's Zurich branch, so I moved there with him as befitting a good Frau. While house hunting, we stayed in a leased home, and then one day we found ourselves pulling into the driveway of the Château Algonquin. After getting out of the vehicle, I glanced up and felt the same shivers that had swept over me the first time I encountered Erwin. This time it was a home, my ideal house, that I fell in love with at first sight. The neglected lakeside home looked terrible, but upon closer inspection I realized its problems were mostly superficial. Seeing it gave me immediate inspiration, and I couldn't wait to get started making it lovely. I spent the first fifty years of my life in the United States. In the second part, I want to reside in Europe, as I explained to Harper's Bazaar. At long last, I had returned to my own place.

Why did I like my time there? Everything! Switzerland is not Tennessee, but when I visit the Swiss countryside, I am reminded of the beautiful scenery I experienced as a child. The cities fascinate me because of the well-preserved architecture that can be found in them. I have noticed the cleanliness of the nation everywhere I have gone. Simply inhaling in the air is like taking in a cool, clean sip of water.

I also like the different nature of each season. The leaves fall off the trees and then return the next year. As a kid, I just assumed it was true because of how easy it seemed. However, in many areas of the globe, people have lost touch with nature's tempo. A true winter, complete with chilly, crisp air and a blanket of snow, exists here. Our town's ice rink is straight out of a vintage postcard, and it's a lot of fun to skate there in the winter.

While I appreciate Switzerland for its beautiful landscapes, the nation also has many other features that draw me there. In Switzerland, a law is a law, and I respect that. To be clear, the sign reading "No Speeding" implies just that. If you drive recklessly and in violation of the law, you might lose your license. You know exactly where you stand since the rules are quite clear. Oh, and the Swiss are always on time, which is something I had to do to become more like. Someone gently reprimanded me for being "fashionably late" to a gathering when I first got here, stating that as a star, I couldn't get away with being late. I didn't need a second explanation.

American politeness is second to none. Before doing business, individuals are expected to contact with one another with pleasantries like "Good morning" or "Good afternoon" at the grocery store, the gas station, or anywhere else. Americans are notoriously impatient, and as a result, they often overlook or discard little courtesies. I once blurted out to Erwin, "Answer the door!" as I heard the doorbell ring. He was deeply hurt by that. Maybe I should have asked my sweetheart, "Darling, would you please answer the door?" That's precisely how I'd put it if the bell rung again. The quality of life for all people is greatly enhanced when people are courteous and caring in their words and deeds.

Thankfully, the Swiss have a long history of treating visitors like family. We have a fantastic group of friends that Erwin and I have established over the years, and there is nothing "show business" about our life here at the Château Algonquin. The basic truth is that Switzerland has always been a place where I feel safe, secure, and content.

In the late '90s, I started making the trip to Europe with my mother, sister, and two boys whenever we all wanted to be together. Yet, these get-togethers didn't always go well. No matter how mature we become, how much self-assurance and success we achieve, there will always be a part of us that wonders, "What does my mother think of me?" My mother's apathy hurt, even though I pretended in my matter-of-fact manner that it didn't. while I was young, she abandoned me, and while I was with Ike, she denied my gift. It didn't change the way I treated her; it just wasn't in me. Nonetheless, I had a firm grasp on who she was and her bounds. I spent my whole childhood knowing that she didn't feel the way a mother should about her kid.

When Ike came into our life, Muh thought of him as the universe coming together. To her, he was the famous one, the brains behind our financial and professional success. Even when his negative conduct was happening in front of her eyes, she still couldn't see it. She certainly didn't attribute any good success we've had to me. She said I should have been thankful that Ike didn't get rid of me. Muh was instrumental in assisting Ike in locating me when I attempted to evade capture. She sided with him no matter what. After all, he was her landlord since he owned the home where she was living. Even after we ended our marriage, Muh continued seeing Ike. His title as "son-in-law" never left her lips. I wasn't interested in hearing the specifics, but I did learn that they maintained contact.

She was on "Team Ike" until my success became too great for her to ignore. The mother of a famous child went on the Tina Turner tour because she cherished the role more than anything. She felt obligated to sit at the head of the table whenever we dined out together, so that everyone could see that she was with Tina. I wished she had shown Anna Mae the same kind of affection.

I took care of her because she was my mother and I could. I eventually purchased her a home in California and had her relocate from St. Louis. She was unhappy with it, so I went out and furnished another one for her. So that she might meet new people while earning some money, I found her a part-time position at a beauty shop. I had to hear all of her gripes and complains. If her Los Angeles kitchen was unclean, I cleaned it for her when I visited. She made a lot of errors, and I rectified them all, even the time she blew the whole air conditioning system in the brand new home I had bought for her. I showed her my world by inviting her to visit my residences in England, France, and Switzerland.

To Muh, it was all irrelevant. She never really believed in my abilities to the point where I could convince her otherwise. She knew so little about me and Erwin when we first met that she immediately blamed him for our tasteful decorating choices. I have no idea how Erwin was able to keep his composure when he gently told her, "Tina is the interior decorator." Not that Erwin has any interest in interior design.

When Muh and my sister Alline came to visit us in the South of France once, tensions were high. Muh was sick at the time. She had to have had twenty different nurses since she was so tough to care for. I felt bad for my sister because now she expected Alline to always look after her, but Alline was being mean to her. Muh was always complaining about something or picking a quarrel with someone. I really want tranquility for us all. My goal was to wake up each day to the stunning panorama of the Mediterranean and feel nothing but bliss. I advised Muh to quit wreaking havoc on the home front. You read the Bible and you claim it's meant to assist you, but it's not helpful if you're arguing with Alline all the time, I told her.

And with that, I'm at a loss for words. She was preparing a retaliatory blow, but I resolved to fix our strained mother-daughter relationship once and for all. I answered, "Muh," meaning no more debate. You may either modify your attitude and try to make up with Alline, or I'll have someone take you back to California. In this condition, you must leave. My explanation made sense to her. She realized I was serious and knew she had to right her crooked ways if she wanted to keep flying. There were no more complaints after that.

In 1999, I lost my mother.

Because of the friendship we never had but so desperately needed, her passing hit me hard. After giving it some thinking, I decided to skip her church service since I felt that my mom deserved all the attention on her special day. Some people in the media took offense at my choice and wrote horrible things about how arrogant I must be to not attend my mother's funeral. This, of course, was not the situation. I didn't want the event to be a photo op for me and a performance for the crowd, who would pay no attention to Muh.

Not so with Ike, however. He reportedly volunteered to drive my family to church and was turned down by Alline, according to my sister. It upset me because one of the plaques referred to him as Muh's "cherished son-in-law." Unfortunately, his appearance that day led to the "Ike and Tina" tabloid headlines I had sought to avoid.

I traveled in for a private funeral shortly after the ceremony ended. After having my mother cremated, I had the whole family join me on a boat off the California coast so that we may scatter her ashes at sea. Ike was, of course, not invited.

My thoughts often return to my mom and grandma. I was having a reading with a psychic one day when I suddenly became acutely aware of their presence. There were ghosts there, the psychic said; she overheard my grandmother and mother talking (argumentatively, most likely) and Mama Georgie saying to Muh, "You know you didn't treat Ann right." My mother responded defensively, "I tried." My grandma retorted angrily, "Well, you didn't try hard enough," clearly not going to let her off the hook. Mama Georgie was not ready to let Muh forget that she wasn't a decent mother to me, not even in the afterlife.

Motherhood is a challenging role. As children, we have idealized notions of how our parents should act, and it's disheartening when they fall short. Having a stay-at-home parent would have been great for my kids, I know that. Unfortunately, it wasn't the case. We were always on the move, and Ike's inner demons had a chilling effect on the boys as they were developing. These included his unbridled ambition, his drug abuse, his fury, and the violence that often accompanied it. They saw our constant bickering and my bloodshot eyes. While none of Ike's kids responded, my sensitive and emotional eldest son, Craig, was very concerned. Craig came to check on me once when Ike was being really hostile, asking, "Mother, are you all right?" Oh, this can't happen in the home! was my first thinking. I didn't want my kids to overhear or see anything like that. I had anticipated that they would be moved by it, and they were. The effects of Ike's actions on everyone of us were unique.

As the mother of four sons, I naturally wanted the best for them and did my best as a parent. One day I looked at them and said, "You know what? I'm not going to take care of you anymore. I want you to become self-sufficient. I thought teaching children to fend for themselves would serve them more than any material gift I could offer them. A lot of bad things have happened to them. Most of my time has been spent with Craig, who, like a baby, appears to cry whenever our visit comes to an end. Some emotions stay with you forever.

Since he was a teenager, Ronnie and I have butted heads over the fact that he claims to be the only "real" one, the son of both Ike and Tina. He followed in his father's footsteps by engaging in risky behavior and drug use (addictions often run in families). A series of unpaid parking tickets from his wilder days led to his arrest. They locked him in, and to his amazement, he discovered Ike in the same cell. How likely is that, exactly? Ike spotted an opportunity when he found out that Ronnie would be making his bed and cleaning up after him. The good news is that Ronnie took what happened to him as a lesson. He needed to take control of his life if he didn't want to wind up like his father, which he stated he didn't. As a musician, he has to deal with the pressure of living in his parents' shadow.

After the divorce, Ike Jr. and Michael stopped spending time with me. I will not assume to narrate their lives on their behalf. But I would admit that I never wanted the boys to be financially reliant on me, since I considered that a certain way to weaken them. I used to make the joke, "I'm not the Valley Bank." They need to rely on their own arms and legs for balance, just like I did.

After taking some time off from performing in the early 2000s, I signed up for the Twenty Four Seven Millennium Tour. This was supposed to be my last tour, so I planned a whirlwind run around Europe and North America to deliver on every want of my fans. After 44 years in the business, I decided to call it quits and let my finest work speak for itself in people's memories. I was excited to do it again and committed to making it a memorable performance.

When I moved up to touring venues, I was able to expand my performances both conceptually and in terms of staging. When I first started performing on stage, I felt like I was in a movie and I no longer felt the draw to become an actor on film. Each performance was like a mini- or full-length film, complete with an ensemble cast (including myself, my dancers, and the band), a massive backstage support staff, and eye-popping visuals. The architect Mark Fisher, whose resume includes the sets for such acts as Pink Floyd, the Rolling Stones, U2, and Lady Gaga, really excelled with this gigantic show, which included spectacular visual effects.

The "Claw," a sixty- to eighty-foot cantilevered arm that lifted me out over the crowd, was the main attraction and almost killed Roger during every concert. I hung over the railing to get closer to the people, so near that I could see their faces and gaze directly into their eyes, and they could see me as I danced on the tiny platform on my heels, sometimes seeming to slip just a bit to make Roger uneasy. That shared experience was beautiful.

After the exhausting Twenty Four Seven tour, I was ready for a lengthy rest, if not a permanent one. I've never been one to be unable to kick back and unwind. Even though I like silence, my job is rather loud. When I wasn't working, how did I pass the time? I could have gone without music. I like reading, meditating, having meaningful conversations with Erwin, and watching horror movies, the more terrifying the better. As a result of my career in performance, I am now a definite night owl. Erwin and I still have trouble waking up early and often stay up until the small hours of the morning. At the entrance of the Château Algonquin is a big metal sign reading, "No deliveries before noon."

Our modest rural cottage is one of our favorite places to go to when we have some free time. There's a great phrase for the faraway place where the home is situated. The locals have given it the name "wo sich Fuchs und Hase gute Nacht sagen," which translates to "where the fox and the rabbit say good night." The same as "nowhere," if you will. That's OK with us. Having nothing to do and nowhere to go. We use the automobile as our confessional when we go to the country. I think all couples would benefit greatly from a trip like this. Erwin drives while I sit in the passenger seat and we have a wide-ranging conversation about anything and everything. No matter the topic, we provide it without any omissions or censorship. Erwin often says, "There are no secrets in the cockpit." The Dalai Lama is the source of this information. The concept that conflict is beneficial is what's good, not the automobile. There was one thing he stressed, though: "One thing," he remarked, "always do confrontation. The longer you bottle up your emotions, the worse off you'll be. Erwin began to relax after hearing it. Our discussions sometimes become hot, and it usually takes me a while to calm down since I'm an emotional wreck. In any case, we work things out via conversation. We've learned the hard way that compromise is essential to every healthy partnership. My terrible connection with Ike has ironically helped me value and nurture my wonderful friendship with Erwin.

After all these years, this is the one taboo subject? Decorating. No amount of time spent in the automobile will ever end the decorating wars, particularly in the country. I wondered whether I would ever feel at ease in the country home when I first began spending time there. I coaxed Erwin into going furniture shopping with me, and while we were out I'd ask, "Darling, do you like this?" about each item. Erwin would always appear to agree, pull the plug, and place an order that was diametrically opposed to mine. Erwin found solace in his home, a place where he could be himself, unfussy and macho. After some internal debate, I settled on, "Okay, Tina. You've accumulated quite the estate. Stand back. His possession. Just give it to him. The problem is that it was (and still is) very challenging.

Erwin has an extensive collection of power tools since he enjoys working with his hands. He has a state-of-the-art garage and is interested in everything that moves with the help of an engine. Erwin considers racing to be a sport. He often takes weeklong road trips with other automobile and motorbike enthusiasts, and he's constantly trying to convince me of the joys of such excursions. It's a ride, I tell them. Indeed, this is a thoroughfare. The object is a motor vehicle. So what makes it so exceptional?" But Erwin claims it's a fraternity, full of the type of strong bonds that last even the worst times. He claims that motorcyclists are fundamentally wonderful individuals who have been unfairly stereotyped. The only thing I know for sure is that he will come back from these outings smelling like gas. And then there was the time he had a little issue when he returned from the "Mille Miglia" event in Italy. The exhaust had heated the floor of the 1951 red Ferrari 340 America racing vehicle to the point that the rubber sole of Erwin's Timberland shoe melted off. To get around, he taped it up using gaffer's tape. That's commitment! Even though I make fun of him, I admire Erwin's dedication to his hobbies. During this time, I went through a period of relative calm during which the Google search query "Did Tina Turner die?" may have reached its peak in popularity. In 2005, I was honored at the Kennedy Center in Washington, D.C., putting to rest any speculation about my whereabouts. At first I refused it because I couldn't fathom what I might have done to merit such an honor; I'd always thought of myself as someone who just got out of bed and went to work. But I put on my finest Galliano and sat amongst the other awardees like Robert Redford, Tony Bennett, Julie

Harris, and Suzanne Farrell, listening to everyone say such wonderful things about me. Even President George W. Bush said that I had the most famous legs in show industry. I saw Al Green, Queen Latifah, and Melissa Etheridge all sing my songs, and they were all fantastic in their own ways, but Al Green and Queen Latifah were my favorites. However, Beyoncé was the true show-stopper that night. She walked out on stage in a dress that Bob Mackie had originally made for me (he still had a second one in his archives) and said, "Every now and again, when I think of inspiration, I think of the two Tinas in my life—that is, my mother, Tina, and of course, the magnificent Tina Turner. When I first watched you perform, I was blown away. Never have I seen a lady so strong and fearless. The sincerity of her remarks moved me deeply. She broke out into a rendition of "Proud Mary." Let me tell you, her performance set the stage ablaze. The whole crowd was up and dancing the whole time. All eyes were on me as they waited to hear my reaction to hearing someone else sing my song. Yes, please! Beyoncé was so ferocious and powerful, and I couldn't wait to tell her that in the dressing room.

Like everyone else of my age, I was excited to meet Caroline Kennedy that night; upon seeing her, my thoughts immediately went to her mother and how much she meant to me. I was still profoundly affected by the old Kennedy charisma. I sprang to my feet and yelled, "I came because of you!" with the same fervor I had felt all those years ago when I first laid eyes on Jackie in that hotel lobby. It was worth it everything to meet Caroline again and hear her kind voice asking about my life. She told the story of how I became a famous singer. She continued, "But," she said, "when Tina takes the wig off, the darkness comes."

But the clouds were beginning to part. When I heard in 2007 that Ike had died of a cocaine overdose, the recollection seemed so far away that it was almost unreal. The children had already told me that Ike's life was difficult. He never managed to dig himself out of his drug addiction, incarceration, or pursuit of a hit song. The burden of his misery was too great, and he gave up the ghost. A tragic tale, really.

Naturally, I was inundated with inquiries from the media in the hopes that I would make a comment and provide fodder for a headline. But I remained mute and detached out of respect. It was as though Ike had never been. It was like hearing about a long-lost friend, one I hadn't seen in over thirty years. When I realized I was emotionless, I knew I had successfully moved on.

I spent my time in Switzerland working on a musical project to satisfy my creative needs while on holiday. As part of her Beyond project, my friend Regula Curti asked me to join her in documenting Christian and Buddhist prayers that overlap and are linked. Working with Regula to record Beyond (a total of four CDs) allowed me to vocalize my spirituality via chanting, which was and remains a significant part of my life. Since I was interested in spreading some kind of spiritual message but was at a loss as to what that message should be, I decided to see Deepak Chopra. The two of us, Erwin and I, went to California's Chopra Center to consult with Deepak. It gave me some great ideas. One of the lessons I wanted to convey to the Beyond audience was,

"Start every day singing like the birds—singing takes you beyond, beyond, beyond, beyond."

I know I claimed the Twenty Four Seven tour was my last and that I was retiring after that. However, a couple events transpired that caused me to rethink my choice. I was honored to share the stage with Beyoncé to sing "Proud Mary" at the 2008 Grammys. She speaks her mind and has a powerful presence that sets her apart. Having pleasure singing and dancing with her reminded me of the times I spent with my dancers. Being able to be as wicked as I wanted onstage with my girlfriends was the nicest part of my work on occasion. It made me wonder whether I had missed anything. A little amount at least?

Later, during an Armani fashion show in Milan, I happened to be seated close to Sophia Loren. We got to chatting about our recent activities, and I brought up the fact that I've been taking a vacation from singing. She questioned, "How long?" To which I replied, "Oh, about seven years," to which she snapped, "Break over!" Your presence is desired. "Everyone, back to work!"

After making an appearance on the Grammys, I began to get more fan letters than normal. I walked about collecting tiny messages from strangers, sometimes written on napkins. I kept every single one and soon had quite a stack. After that, I decided to phone Roger and tell him, "It's time for one last tour." I was ready to leave "retirement" at age 69 and hit the road again. My half century (wow, that's a long time) as a performer would be appropriately commemorated by a tour titled "Fiftieth Anniversary." My first professional gig was with Ike and the Kings of Rhythm in Missouri, so that's where we wanted to get things off.

When we arranged our opening night in Kansas City, some dimwitted executive decided that it would be a bad idea for me to walk out on the "Claw" when I performed "Nutbush" because of the insurance risks involved. He probably misjudged my age and assumed I couldn't hold my footing. "Fine," Roger said, "but who's going to tell Tina?" Nobody, that's who; nobody had the guts to tell Tina. Hanging out above the crowd, I danced my heart out on that Claw while chanting, "Nutbush one more time!" That was one of the times I feigned intoxication.

I looked forward to going back to the office. Nonetheless, I was aware of the fact that my vigor wasn't what it once was. Considering the grueling schedule of my foreign tour and my advanced age, fatigue was to be anticipated. I also had to deal with the effects of high blood pressure. My diagnosis came in 1978, and I didn't give it much thought at the time. My mother and sister both had it, therefore it must run in the family. For some reason, I was never fully explained the dangers of hypertension. I accepted it at its value, as if having "high" blood pressure was the norm for me, and thus didn't stress about bringing it down. In 1985, I went to the doctor and he prescribed me medicine that I took once a day.

There were evenings when I had to force myself to get in the mood while I applied my makeup. Despite the fatigue, aches, and tiredness I felt in the dressing room, when I went out onto that stage I was Tina, and the audience saw the Tina they wanted to see. But I was aware of the distinction. Every song I sing is a chance for me to spread my wings and fly. It was more and more difficult to shift into second gear and fly the way I was used to with each performance.

I thought my high blood pressure and the medicine were causing my body to have an adverse reaction, and that was why I was having trouble hitting my notes. Dammit! I aimed for that harmony. No matter what was holding me back, I had to overcome it, and it required all I had to get through my show each night. After each performance, Roger would enter my dressing room and give me a strange look, as if he sensed that I was too exhausted to continue.

I came down with a terrible chest cold halfway through the trip. After rescheduling a few gigs, we settled on May 5th, 2009, in Sheffield, which is in Yorkshire and is approximately three hours north of London. Claire, my main dancer, is from Sheffield, so naturally we had a blast dancing there. I hoped that everyone who went there would have a fantastic time. Those who were there will never forget Tina Turner's last performance. Fans still come up to me now, years after the Fiftieth Anniversary tour finished, and tell me how much they appreciated it. I estimate that over a million people in North America and Europe saw the tour.

I returned to the hotel once the last show ended. I kept my voice down. This was the last straw for me. The next morning, Erwin and I checked in for our flight and I didn't see a single anybody, not even Roger. I just sat there, still and collected and determined. To myself, I murmured, "I'm not going back."

I hope no one takes this the wrong way, but I was ready to call it quits after many years of hard effort. I knew now was the time to do it if I wanted my followers to leave with a positive last impression of me. I didn't want people to come to a concert a year or two from now and say, Oh, she used to be excellent. I took enormous satisfaction in myself, and I also had impeccable timing. There's a saying that goes something like, "Leave the party before it's over." After a long night of dancing to "Proud Mary," I was ready to go home and put away my dance shoes.

EXTENDED CATASTROPHE

And now that you're retired, what are you going to do with your time? The main idea is to avoid doing anything at all, whether out of necessity or by design. To be alone with my belongings at home was a top priority for me. I yearned to go grocery shopping, stroll with Erwin, tend to my garden and feel the earth under my fingers, see the changing of the seasons near the lake, and, above all, relax in peace. Although I don't need music, there are certain songs that make me want to sing along. The Chainsmokers and Coldplay's "Something Just Like This" ("doo-doo-doo, doo-doo-doo, doo-doo-doo, doo-doo-doo, doo-doo-doo") is what I'm listening to right now. I find it really appealing.

When I informed Mick I was retiring, I saw him at a gig shortly after my last tour, and I had the impression he wanted to scold me. The only time I can recall him being quiet and not quickly retaliating was when I questioned, "Mick, do you ever get tired?" He remained silent for quite some time. Even though I knew the answer was yes, he'd never admit it. He does things his own way. As long as he is able to walk, I believe he will remain outside. Which is totally OK. He's Mick Jagger, lead singer for the Rolling Stones, and he rocks.

Retiring was immediately enjoyable for me. Not only did I not look my age, but I also felt great. My body was always the result of my effort, all those years of dancing. For the last fifty years, I've been doing the hardest stage exercises known to man, and I credit it for keeping me in such great shape. However, I can boast that I have never touched narcotics or cigarettes. Unless I have to be somewhere at a certain time, I like to sleep in for at least eight hours. I take my time now days because I appreciate the finer things in life.

There must be something I'm doing right, since in 2013 I was requested to appear on the cover of German Vogue. At the ripe old age of seventy-three, I believe it is fair to claim that I held the record for oldest "girl" on a Vogue cover. I felt like I was making a powerful statement for women of all ages as I posed with my hands on my hips in a magnificent blue Giorgio Armani gown for photographers Claudia Knoepfel and Stefan Indlekofer. When I was on stage, I used to joke that I didn't give any regard to my audience's age. I didn't age at all. The way I am now living makes me feel the same way. Taking care of oneself on the inside and out will allow your inner and outside beauty and joy to shine through. It doesn't matter what the number is.

But as you get older, you'll reach a point when you want to take charge and must begin making plans. I made the choice to weed out the extraneous from my existence. Since I've found such contentment in Switzerland, I've had to sell a few possessions, including my lovely home in the South of France. And then my mind turned to Erwin. We were inseparable in every manner save the law for twenty-six years. Because he was the person I cared about most on this earth, it seemed unjust that he would have no recourse or legal standing in the event of my death. We were both aware that we needed to take action.

In 2012, while on a tour around the Greek islands, Erwin asked me to marry him, and I happily accepted. In addition, I applied for Swiss citizenship to further demonstrate my dedication to our future together in Switzerland. I don't want anybody to think that giving up my American passport was a hasty or impulsive move on my part. It was deliberate and deliberate. I will never let go of the part of me that was born in the United States and identifies as such. But after meeting Erwin and moving to Europe, everything changed. There were less and fewer reasons for me to visit the United States as the years went by. In 2010, I lost my dearest sibling, Alline. My boys are grown men now with busy schedules, but I'm always available by phone or aircraft if they need me. Since I was already living in Switzerland and had done so for over two decades, it made natural for me to consider that nation my permanent residence.

Let me tell you, becoming a citizen of a nation is a lot harder than being one from the start. I had to go through a challenging exam, so I studied with a tutor. High German, the most proper (and challenging) version of the language, was among the many things I had to study. The next step was to present myself to a panel that would assess my qualifications. When I inquired whether Erwin could come along to my interview, I was informed that only the applicant was allowed.

When I came in, there were seven judges sitting at tables. Before millions of people, I never once felt nervous, but in front of this bunch, I was absolutely petrified. To lighten the mood, I quickly confessed that I was, in fact, rather anxious. There was a total lack of reply. Then, in a last-ditch effort, I distributed some candy that I had specifically bought for the event, because, let's face it, who doesn't enjoy sugar? And Switzerland in particular. I thought, "Tina, the candy isn't working either," when there was still no response. The group was clearly committed to doing a good job. I was all by myself.

A deep spoken guy replied, "Tina, do you realize that you have to speak the language before you can apply for citizenship?"

I said "yes," hoping for a positive response. "In High German, I can introduce myself, tell you where I come from, and count the number of my offspring." Kind of. I could give it a go, and if I got stuck, I could look up the solutions in a little booklet. Perhaps I was overreacting, but I felt like one of the younger interviewees was gazing at me specifically to increase my anxiety.

With a sigh of relief, I said, "Ich bin Tina Turner."

I had to look forward in the book to find the solution to the following puzzle. It dawned on me to finally ask, "May I?" It's "Darf ich?" My instructor drilled into my head that the Swiss are very polite and that they always need permission before doing anything.

The last question proved to be the most challenging. To paraphrase, "Can you tell us something you know about Switzerland?"

I couldn't think of anything until I recalled that, at a party not so long ago, someone had been discussing the "Schweizerpsalm," the Swiss national hymn. One listener likened it to a hymn rather than a usual nationalistic anthem, and indeed, "Schweizerpsalm" literally translates to "Swiss psalm." I improvised my response to center on this idea. I confidently said, "I am learning the national anthem, and I find it interesting that it sounds so religious, like something you would hear in a church."

The reporter was shocked. The national anthem is the most revered piece of music in the country, yet he never expected Tina Turner to bring it up. He would have been just as unsurprised if I had begun talking about DJ BoBo, a Swiss rock artist. It turned out to be the best solution possible. A song has rescued me from peril once again. My application was accepted by the committee, and I now have a Swiss passport.

My new citizenship seems to pique the curiosity of many individuals outside myself for some reason. So much noise was made, and so much conjecture was made, that many began to believe I must have done it to avoid paying taxes. Living in a nation for seventeen years with the person you love, particularly when that person is going to become your spouse, is reason enough to call that country home.

I don't know whether I've done our wedding justice by describing it, but I hope the memories are still vivid in your memory as they are in mine. The intoxicating fragrance of the blossoms remains even when I shut my eyes. I'm sure I'm not the only bride who has watched her wedding DVD several times, but each time I do, I see something new.

The next day, Erwin and I continued our fairytale by jetting out to the Grand Hotel a Villa Feltrinelli on Italy's Lake Garda for our honeymoon. Garlands of "just married" flowers, a lovely, traditional touch for a mature couple, were placed on the front of the vehicle as we drove there. Thankfully, it didn't rain the day before, but now that it has, the flowers are too heavy to carry and we've had to stop. The hotel's boathouse, which we had to ourselves, was the ideal setting for our honeymoon.

When we visited Oprah in the South of France at the famed Grand-Hôtel du Cap-Ferrat to film a series of interviews for Oprah's Next Chapter, we swapped one stunning setting for another.

It would take Oprah to get a newlywed to call off her honeymoon. Partially because we had so much fun together, and partly because I wanted to have one final conversation about my old life before beginning my new one as Mrs. Erwin Bach, I consented. I was ready to talk about anything, even my time with Ike, in the hopes of finally putting the whole affair to rest.

I told Oprah firmly that I had spent the previous two years planning, organizing, and preparing, outlining the factors that led to my retirement, downsizing frenzy, and resolve to prioritize what mattered most. I said I was finally in charge of my own life. Does the saying "If you want to make God laugh, tell him your plans" ring a bell? The term "control" is the last thing I would use to describe what happened to me, so that's what comes to mind when I think back on it. Three months after the wedding, on a normal October morning when I was supposed to be leaving for a holiday in Marrakesh with some friends, I was hit with a sobering reminder of my own mortality.

When I finally opened my eyes, I attempted to speak, but no sounds came out. Erwin, who never loses his composure in a crisis, saw that something was very wrong and promptly phoned my doctor, Professor Doctor Vetter, who instructed him to give me an aspirin and take me to the emergency room. To my chagrin, I continued convincing myself that everything was alright. Even though a wheelchair was waiting for me when I arrived at the hospital, I first refused to use it. It wasn't until the doctor recommended that I use it that I finally gave in. When the orderlies laid me down on a table and covered me with a blanket, I knew we weren't heading to Marrakesh after all. I had no idea the severity of my situation until it was too late.

Just keep denying it.

I was so unaware that when I realized I was alone in the room, I got up and left. I flung my legs over the edge of the desk and crashed to the floor below. That's when I realized I needed help to survive. What the heck am I doing, God? As if I were to blame for my own demise, I told myself. My next thought was, "How do I get rid of this?" I didn't know the answers, and I was too ashamed to ask for assistance. Despite having danced for hours and having strong legs, I was unable to get up. I limped up to a couch and forced myself to sit down, thinking the whole time that there's no way Tina Turner could ever be paralyzed. A sleepy state overtook me and I eventually passed out. The next day, Professor Doctor Vetter informed me that I had suffered a stroke. I listened to him this time. The impact of the stroke on my body was significant. Everything on my right side became numb. He told me that using my right hand would be difficult, and that I would need to work with a physiotherapist to learn how to walk again. If I fell, I had to learn a unique technique for getting back up. I realized I would be knocked down quite a bit.

When we first begin to walk, we are often carefree, adventurous youngsters who are brimming with confidence due to their lack of experience with the challenges that life inevitably presents. When you're an adult and you have to learn how to walk, you realize the consequences of falling are never good. It's also a source of shame. I was feeling drained and hopeless. I really questioned whether or not I would ever be able to dance in high heels again.

I was in the hospital for approximately a week, and I managed to bring myself back together during that period. I am resilient; I told myself. I've always been this way. I vowed that I would never give up trying to rehabilitate my leg and get it walking so that I could finally stand on my own two feet. I forced myself to act since I've had to constantly drive myself forward. Although successful, the process of recovery was far from simple.

Though I wanted to give all of my attention to healing, I had to keep tabs on international events. There were whispers going around. "Tina Turner Is Doing Fine After Suffering a Stroke." Tina Turner Is Sick, But No One Knows What It Is. If word got out, the cameras would be all over me, and worried fans would form a vigil outside my house. Although I was aware that tabloid photographers would fight to get a shot of me in my current state, my motivation was not vanity. The interruption was too much for me to bear. It would add another issue to my plate, at a time when I already felt overwhelmed. Everything you said, I said wasn't true. We kept it a secret.

Traditional Chinese medicine (TCM) helped me get back on my feet a few weeks after my stroke, while I was still rehabilitating under the care of my physicians. The incident altered my appearance and gait. My Traditional Chinese Medicine (TCM) therapist, Sylvie Ackerman, recommended regular acupuncture sessions, focusing on the face. Like a battery, the yin and yang energy of the body must be kept in equilibrium for TCM to be effective, I was taught. Because I pay close attention to how I feel, I was able to track every improvement and change that occurred as a result of my sessions. What I did I referred to as "taking little, wonderful steps back in life." After seeing the positive effects of TCM, I decided to include it into my routine.

Nonetheless, my stroke would have lasting bodily consequences. I still have trouble producing a readable signature, so signatures are out of the question. But maybe much more significant were the consequences on people's minds. After the ceremony on my wedding day, I first became aware that something was wrong with my body. I had been experiencing pain in my neck and chest. The pain wasn't severe, and it disappeared as abruptly as it had been, but I began to wonder if it was a portent. Which suggests what? Age? An extreme health issue? A stroke was something that should happen to an elderly, ill person, not me, and suddenly I'd had one.

Sadness consumed me. I have no strength or energy because of the fight to become well. It wasn't simply the effects of the stroke that I was coping with. My primary care physician sent me to a nephrologist because he was worried about the effects of my high blood pressure on my kidneys. Expert nephrologist Dr. Jörg Bleisch told me that my kidneys were barely functioning at 35% of normal. He recommended extra medicine to keep my high blood pressure under control and expressed concern, saying we would have to watch them closely.

I started the next episode of what would turn out to be a very lengthy health soap opera while still reeling from the devastating news of my failing kidneys. I was on holiday in Greece when the latest crisis began, exactly one year after my stroke. Seeing the traditional Greek environment brought to life was exciting for me since I like movies like Clash of the Titans and tales about gods, monsters, and Greek mythology. I had been admiring the ancient ruins when all of a sudden I felt weak, lightheaded, and queasy. I was knocked off my feet by the intensity of the feeling.

It was terrifying to learn that I suffer from vertigo, or what the Swiss term "Schwindel," an acute kind of imbalance. Tina, who had scaled the Eiffel Tower and performed a dance atop a moving crane, periodically feigning a fall to see the horrified reaction of her manager (sorry, Roger), now felt queasy simply holding her head up. I was unable to keep my balance or concentrate. In fact, I saw movement of any type as a threat. My body and my world were both whirling wildly out of control.

This was a completely new illness, and I needed medical attention immediately. Fortunately, I was residing in a nation that boasts the greatest healthcare system in the whole world. The study of vertigo, which is commonly misdiagnosed as "dizziness" and remains mostly uncharted in many parts of the world, is a significant focus of research at Zurich, which is conveniently located in my immediate vicinity. The neurologist at the Interdisciplinary Center for Vertigo and Neurological Visual Disorders, Professor Doctor Dominik Straumann, was tasked with examining me. The doctors determined that the source of my suffering was a small crystal (technically known as a "otoconia") that had been dislodged from its anchoring position deep inside my ear canal.

There's probably a better scientific reason, but my physicians settled on the chair as my kind of therapy. We went down into the basement of the school by a secret passage. A joke I made upon first seeing the chair was, "Is this where Frankenstein's monster sits?" It was a huge piece of machinery that might have fit in at NASA or on a roller coaster from the future, and it looked like it had been plucked straight from a laboratory. They must think I'm crazy if they expect me to go in here and ride it. My doctor and his two aides put me into the chair, fastened the straps, and activated the device.

The "chair" in question, I'm informed, is really a three-dimensional turntable that acts as a three-axis stimulator. It can rotate in any axis, making 360-degree rotations. The aim, in my instance, was to reposition the errant crystal that was giving me vertigo. The physicians assured me that once that happened, the dizzying illness would cease. My eyes were wide open as I was strapped to the machine and spun about in all directions as the physicians studied my irises to see whether the therapy was having any effect. They kept saying, "Don't move, Tina," which was a bit strange given that most people anticipate my next move.

But trust me, comedy was the last thing on my mind as I was being cuffed to that chair. The sickness I experienced was so profound it reached all the way to my spirit. For many sessions, I returned to the chair, and each time I wondered, "How did I ever survive that?" My spirit was broken. I was too ill to make the short drive home, so Erwin had to leave me overnight in the clinic.

The day the enigmatic crystal finally reacted to the chair's zero-gravity swings and settled into place meant the end of my dizziness. I spent about a month in a wheelchair since the surgery exhausted me so much. Once it threatened to return, but I mustered all my power and fought it off with all I had. As soon as I recognized the symptoms of an episode, I did my best to remain immobile, Schwindel's demonic presence always looming in the background with the threat, "If you move the wrong way, I'm coming." As I struggled to ignore the feeling, I found myself breaking out in a cold sweat. It was like looking straight into the eyes of a dog that warns, "If you move, I'll bite you." I resisted, determined to make it stop.

The victory made me feel good, but I failed to anticipate the greater challenges that were ahead. Constant struggles that would leave me wondering how I went from being the image of health, a cover girl, a bride for God's sake, to Job.

As Dr. Bleisch worked to lower my blood pressure, I became more conscious that something was amiss with my kidneys. I looked into the kidneys to learn their function. Something that, if I'm being really candid, I had never considered before. Unless they're in the midst of a serious health emergency, I doubt most individuals can name their internal organs or explain what they perform.

Remember, we were both speaking different languages. Due of my limited German language skills, the physicians were forced to communicate with me in English, a language that was obviously strange to them. It wasn't simple, but they were really patient and accomplished a lot.

The kidneys are the filtering organs of the body, and they cleanse around 450 liters of blood per day. Waste items are extracted from the circulation and finally expelled in urine by a highly intricate process involving filtering units called glomeruli. When everything is running well, we don't even notice it. However, the body might run into difficulties if the kidneys are unable to filter out excess waste, salt, or moisture.

In such a case, "renal replacement therapy," which might include dialysis or a kidney transplant, becomes necessary. A kidney transplant is the best option here. One healthy kidney can do the job of two unhealthy ones. A transplanted kidney greatly improves a patient's chances of living a normal life. People who have had kidney transplants tend to live longer and feel better than those who are on dialysis.

Dialysis, in the form of hemodialysis or peritoneal dialysis, is another alternative. Hemodialysis is the most common method, and it is performed in a clinic or hospital setting. Going to a facility where a machine removes waste and surplus fluid from the blood three times weekly for around four hours at a time.

To be fair, I can't say for sure how much of this I was really processing at the time. It's easy to tune out physicians' advice while you're unwell, whether out of fear, resistance, or outright denial. I didn't believe I was in any imminent danger even though I was aware of words like "transplant" and "dialysis."

My kidneys were supposed to get better or at least stay stable. Once again, the term "plan" appears. Hold up there, Tina. When plans are discussed, you know what will happen. It generally foreshadows a surprise, and sure enough, one was coming. Another medical issue, and this one was serious, came as a complete surprise to me. I had been dealing with the taboo illness of persistent diarrhea for months. Because of my extreme fatigue and the unpredictability of my condition, I had to stop going out in public. In fact, I barely made it down from the second story. I had to muster all my energy just to make it from my bedroom to the bathroom. I looked dreadful and felt like a prisoner. A shadow of my former self. When I needed help the most, Erwin was there for me.

Shockingly, in January of 2016, I was told that I had early-stage intestinal cancer, namely a carcinoma and multiple malignant polyps. It was unclear at this time whether or not the cancer could be removed, much alone what would happen next. The days of waiting were the worst. I tiptoed from room to room, becoming stir crazy within. I spent a lot of time staring into space, at the lake, the walls, old photos, and even the piano, which was never played. I begged Erwin, "Aren't you sorry you married an old woman?" since our lives revolved around visits to various medical professionals. Thankfully, he had a positive outlook on life. From the first moment I met him, Erwin had an air of self-assurance, positivity, and a zest for life. I needed his aid to be level-headed amid this terrifying roller coaster.

The best part about roller coasters is that they take you up as well as down. A month following my diagnosis, I had surgery to have the affected section of my intestine removed. Thanks to the early diagnosis, the cancer turned out to be rather slow-growing. After hearing that there was hope for a treatment from my physicians, I started to feel better. However, it was a brief gleam.

My kidneys are failing, Dr. Bleisch said, and we have a serious medical problem. It's never good to hear that you have cancer, but in my situation, it had far-reaching effects. I would need to take medicine to strengthen my immune system if I were diagnosed with cancer. The issue was that in order to prevent the body from rejecting the new organ, the patient had to take "immunosuppressants," medications that have the opposite effect of dampening the immune system. That is to say, the two therapies are incompatible with one another. If my kidneys were to deteriorate to the point where a transplant was necessary, the medications used to manage my cancer would be at odds with the drugs required for a successful transplant.

I never expected to be in such a terrible spot between a rock and a hard place. I always thought that a kidney transplant would be an option in the event of a catastrophic renal failure. After cancer surgery, however, Dr. Bleisch told me it was very improbable. We can't even think about a transplant for at least another year. A year! If only I had a year. Naturally, the most pressing issue was, from whom might I get a kidney in the event that I need one?

Living in Switzerland was of little use to me at this time. At the time, the nation had one of the lowest rates of organ donors (from dead donors) in Europe, so if I joined the waiting list, it would be for an indefinite amount of time. I had reached the ripe old age of 75. How long would I have to wait before I was called? Could I possibly hope for a chance to participate? I was a long shot since I was a lady in her sixties. her condition seemed hopeless since I was a lady in her 70s with cancer. I was once again in a situation where I was buffeted by high winds. It was out of the question to purchase a kidney on the dark web. I never even entertained the thought. But do you really think any famous person would attempt to acquire an organ in secret? Instagram is where it would most likely wind up. In July, my kidneys had weakened to the point that I would need to start dialysis soon. That was a concept I strongly disagreed with. "Oh no, no, no," I yelled at him. As the saying goes, "I'm not a machine." This was not how I saw my life.

But the poisons inside of me had begun to take control. I just wasn't hungry. My whole tummy was covered with little bumps. To put it bluntly, I was just getting by. That's probably what happens when you die; you simply fade away gradually. There is no fear of dying in Buddhism. After all, I told myself, I'm not a youngster anymore. In my younger years, I may have thought, "Oh, I don't want to die because I don't know what's ahead." I'd reached the point in my life when I'd accomplished my mission, so to speak. There isn't much more to life after reaching this age. I could accept death if my kidneys failed and it was my time to leave. I was feeling a little bit exhausted. I'd accompany my mom and sibling back home. It worked out well, too. When the moment is right, the time is right. We all eventually perish. As for me, I was prepared to take it on board.

I wasn't afraid of death per se since I've always been interested in the afterlife, but I was worried about the process. Assisted suicide is permitted in Switzerland, which is one of the country's advantages. A doctor may legally prescribe a fatal medication to a mentally competent patient who is experiencing "unbearable suffering." However, self-injection of the medication is required. My understanding is that a line is opened, an injection or drink is administered, and the curious go to another reality to learn more. This solution seemed like a painless means of addressing a potentially unpleasant issue. Several groups, such as Exit and Dignitas, provide process coordination as a paid service.

For some reason, I decided to become an Exit member.

That's probably when Erwin started to accept the thought that I was dead. He expressed strong feelings about his inability to bear the thought of my going away. He said that he had no desire for either another life or another lady. He would have done everything to preserve our happiness together.

Erwin's sudden offer of a kidney as a donation came as quite a shock.

Even now, there are moments when I have to pinch myself to be sure I'm not dreaming. The scope of his offer really floored me. My first reaction, motivated by my affection for him, was to attempt to dissuade him from taking such a drastic and permanent measure. A young dude, at that. He shouldn't put himself in danger to extend my life because I'm an elderly lady. With just one kidney, he was certain he could make it. What if anything were to happen to him, though? What if he had renal disease down the road? "Honey, you're still young. Please, please, please don't let me in any part of your life. Put yourself first, I advised.

Erwin, though, had already decided. He considered me in his plans for the future. Our future is my future, he assured me. And the prospect of requiring a kidney transplant in the future didn't bother him at all. Giving was a virtue in his eyes. He was self-assured, believing that "if you give, you receive," as the saying goes.

We were holding hands in the living room, gazing out at the lake, when I burst into tears. I opted to think that a kidney transplant was possible, even if my physicians were pessimistic about the prospect. After my stroke, Schwindel, cancer, and now this, I finally felt something that had been lacking from my life for quite some time: hope.

It gave me hope.

QUESTION MY EMOTIONS

Dialysis treatment was essential to maintaining health and, frankly, survival. Even though I knew it was the best and only option, the thought of being permanently attached to a machine made me uncomfortable. During my preliminary visit to the clinic, I told my doctor, "I'm just taking a look at the equipment." Something that looked like R2D2 from Star Wars was staring back at me from the dialysis chamber. My kidneys would be replaced by this little contraption. Should I go through with this? I was curious. I was trapped. It was a chore, not something I looked forward to doing. This was the circuitous route I took to get to a dialysis chair at a Zollikon, Switzerland, hospital.

On my initial visit to the clinic, the doctor explained the process of connecting me to the dialysis machine by inserting a catheter into my chest. One of my first thoughts was, "Well, I can't wear low cuts anymore because there's going to be a hole there!" Even though I felt terrible, I was still Tina, and I never stopped caring about how I looked. Since the catheter would remain in place for the duration of my dialysis treatments, I was warned to take special care to prevent infection at the puncture site. You should also limit your fluid intake and stay away from ill people.

Bright and unadorned (no, I didn't want to repaint it), the dialysis room had its furnishings wrapped in gray plastic for ease of cleaning. The whooshing noise the pumps produced when attached to patients was the most memorable aspect of the space. During dialysis, I also felt an inward whooshing as the fluids were pumped through my body. Like the way one's body might occasionally feel the rhythmic pull of waves after swimming in the water, the feeling lingered for hours after the treatment was over.

There were brighter days and there were bad days. If I felt weak and exhausted after the cleaning procedure because too much water was removed, I would let the nurses know the next time I visited.

I didn't really like my time in the clinic, but I eventually became used to it. The nurses must have loved me because I never acted as they probably thought a celebrity like Tina Turner would: aloof, spoiled, and demanding. They'd be taken aback by how kind you are and exclaim, "Wow. It's understandable that the other patients would complain given their poor health and confinement. But I made an effort to take some levity with me. I didn't think I had any grounds for complaint; after all, my spouse was donating a kidney to me! Even though my list of ailments appeared to grow larger and longer, I kept telling myself that I was fortunate and not doomed.

For the following nine months, I would spend most of my time on the dialysis chair. Maintaining a regular schedule was helpful. Having a fixed routine for my visits to the clinic helped ease my anxiety. Because I was still weak and feeling unwell, I learnt to wear soft, comfy clothing and frequently went into a deep slumber for the first two hours. In the morning, I awoke to the company of Erwin and Didier, our majordomo, the charming guy who manages our home with diligence, talent, and elegance. I read books that were conveniently close at hand and spent the rest of the time fantasizing.

The book of Horst P. Horst's images that I own is one of my most treasured possessions. When I first laid eyes on his framed photographs, I almost lost my balance and fell to the floor in London (I believe I was at Molton Brown). These photos are the most stunning I've ever seen. They embodied everything that is sophisticated and glamorous. I didn't care about the price; I just needed them. I tacked them up in various places and enjoy looking at them often. My house is filled with Horsts, so I took a book of his to the clinic to remind me of them and to tell me that there is still beauty in the world. His finest images include a lady holding a fan, a corseted body viewed from the rear, and a nude draped on a satin curtain.

I am a student of Deepak Chopra's views on awareness and the powerful link between mind and body, thus I have amassed quite a collection of his books. His words have always been an inspiration to me, and meeting him in California only solidified that belief. The concept of confronting mortality may help one develop a true enthusiasm for being alive is one that resonated with me when I was reading The Book of Secrets at the clinic. When I have some free time, I like to go into my chanting room and read what he has to say, taking it all in slowly. I don't know what is ahead in the next life, but I do want to be ready for it, and Deepak Chopra tells us that we must grow extraordinarily to make contact with the unseen parts of the cosmos.

My fascination with Dante is more difficult to articulate, partly because of the greater cognitive challenge he presents. When reading Dante, you must sit quite still. Before starting dialysis, I remember feeling like I was balancing precariously on an eggshell as I read his writings. To fully understand what he was saying about the afterlife, I realized I would have to read his writings more than once. According to The Divine Comedy, we all have to go through hell before we can reach heaven. With knowledge comes advancement to higher levels. Some challenges in life are more noticeable than others. I've been put through my fair share of trials, and I like to believe I've grown as a result, but who knows whether I'll ever achieve the type of enlightenment Dante depicts. Despite how challenging it may be, I'm eager to put myself to the test and attempt it.

Not being in the mood to read caused me to let my thoughts drift wherever they wished. How often must I say,

"I'm done with Ike" before he finally listens? And yet, here I was, musing on long-forgotten recollections, like our wedding in Tijuana and the subsequent trip to a sex show. While sitting in my chair, I was able to reflect, to play back my life like a movie and ask myself the major questions. It's a cliche to say that when you're close to death, you see your whole life flash before your eyes, but that's essentially what occurred to me.

The scenery changed as the current melded with the past. I was thinking about my mom and Ike the whole time I was in the clinic. That Muh had abandoned me and that Ike had assaulted me were facts that could never be hidden. Or maybe it's because I let myself believe for so long that I would never be loved. However, I was beginning to see things from a new angle. In spite of the agony, I understood that my past mistakes did not make up who I am now. My plight turned into a love tale when Erwin entered my life. Whoever denied the sincerity of our feelings would have to acknowledge that Erwin gave me the greatest gift of all: the gift of life.

I was still on medication to manage my hypertension, but I was becoming more resentful of it since I was convinced it was making me feel worse. I longed for the days when I felt like my old self again, when I was mentally sharp and physically active without the aid of drugs. A homeopathic doctor in France was recommended to me by a friend, and I leaped at the opportunity to try something new.

I had trust in a different form of treatment. According to the homeopath, the contaminants in the Château Algonquin's water system were having a negative impact on my health. Since I was willing to try anything once, I had all the pipes in the home rebuilt and some little devices put in so the water could be cleaned using crystals. The new doctor I went to switched me over to homeopathic remedies instead of conventional ones. I found that the purified water was more effective than medication for lowering my blood pressure, and I began drinking it regularly. Perhaps it was hogwash, but I had faith in it, and as I told Erwin, I figured it couldn't harm to give it a try. Since I was afraid my well-respected Swiss physicians wouldn't approve of my drastic tactics, I opted for the easy way out. I just didn't let on that I was trying out other remedies for my hypertension or that I had stopped taking my prescribed medication.

My visit to Dr. Bleisch for a routine exam was the first sign of danger. I wanted to test whether the homeopathic treatments were successful in reducing my blood pressure and enhancing the health of my kidneys after around three months had passed. Since I was feeling OK, I figured the news would be favorable. Not believing it was a huge thing, I told Dr. Bleisch that I had stopped taking my blood pressure medication. A huge blunder. Stupid, stupid, stupid. Clearly taken aback, he was contemplating saying something along the lines of "You have really messed up." But his next question was even more surprising: "Didn't you talk to your other doctors about this?" The doctor warned that discontinuing life-saving medication may have devastating effects on the kidneys.

My doctor informed me that day that my kidneys were permanently damaged because I had neglected to address my high blood pressure, which, as unbelievable as it seems, was something I had not known before. If I'd known then what I know now, my life would have been quite different; for example, I wouldn't have substituted homeopathic remedies for conventional medicine. My lack of knowledge ultimately led to serious repercussions.

The fight against disease is, I realized suddenly, a fight for complete and accurate knowledge. Perhaps I was only trying to secure the stable after the horse had already been taken, but it was crucial that I figure out what had happened to my body so that I could steer clear of such pitfalls in the future. I had no idea, for instance, that kidney disease is known as a "silent killer" because by the time most individuals notice any signs of renal failure, 80 percent of their kidney tissue has already been damaged. High blood pressure, which I have, is a major contributor to renal failure. I may not have had any symptoms at first, but now I realize that many of the issues I attributed to the medicine, such as fatigue, nausea, and itchiness, are really signs of advanced renal disease.

Oh, the many questions I had to myself. I really should have listened to the physicians. What gave me the idea that I could choose how I was treated? If I'd known the consequences of switching to homeopathic remedies, I never would have done it. I don't mean any harm by criticizing homeopathy. After being diagnosed with TB in 1969, I had effective treatment from a homeopathic physician. For a long time, I tried to restore harmony to my system by eliminating stress and purging harmful substances from my blood. It helped me when I was younger, but when I developed a chronic condition that required conventional treatment, homeopathy was no longer a viable option. If only I hadn't stopped taking the drug. If only! A seemingly insignificant choice that would eventually come back to haunt me.

As optimistic as I am, I wanted to know what I might do to reverse the damage done to my kidneys. However, I was informed there was no way to undo the damage I had already done. In December of 2016, my kidney function dropped to an all-time low of 20%. The question, "Does this mean death?" I asked, pausing to allow the obvious response sink in.

In the midst of my deepest shame, remorse, and, yes, sorrow, I discovered something very remarkable about Erwin. Not once did he reprimand me verbally or visually for my error. Instead, he was dependable, kind, and patient. Moreover, he was resolved to assist me in surviving this ordeal.

My kidney function was fast declining, and time was of the essence; thus, the option that had appeared so remote only a short while ago—a kidney transplant—became my only probable salvation. After having a second colonoscopy to be sure no cancerous cells were hiding in my digestive tract, I was given the amazing all-clear. Now that we had Erwin's kidney and didn't have to choose between immunosuppressants and immunoboosters, we could begin planning for the transplant.

There were a number of excellent Swiss hospitals from which Erwin and I might have chosen; ultimately, we decided on one. Friends and reputable professionals all vouched for the University Hospital of Basel, so that's where we went. When we initially went there, I too got a strange sense about it. There, I didn't have to worry about my safety. We were comfortable with everyone we met at the hospital, from the coordinator at Thomas Vögele's office to the surgeon at Professor Doctor Jürg Steiger's office to the doctor in charge of my case at Professor Doctor Gürke's office.

I did some investigating of my own while they were inspecting me, and I was rather taken with what I observed. Professor Doctor Steiger's office included some nice personal touches, such pictures of his kids and a farm scene that turned out to be meaningful to him since it resembled the hilly area where his mother's family had lived. I had the impression that he was a really upbeat and pleasant person, even while talking about extremely serious issues. His demeanour was comforting to me. I felt like he saw me as a full person, not just someone with an illness, when he looked at me.

Both the patient and the donor have a lot on their plates before the transplant even begins, and the real work begins long before the incision is made. The first stage in the lengthy and complicated clearance procedure was Erwin's selfless choice to donate one of his kidneys to me. In Switzerland, "living donor" transplants, in which a healthy individual willingly donates an organ to a patient in need, have accounted for approximately half of all kidney transplants done since the year 2000. There is a tight set of regulations. Before the advent of organ donation banks, the only acceptable live donors were parents, siblings, and children. It wasn't until 1991 that couples or friends who weren't married may give organs to each other.

It was, indeed, crucial that Erwin's kidney be a good match for me, and a battery of tests would establish that. However, the typical clearance procedure also included a battery of psychiatric examinations, known as a "psycho-social evaluation," to ascertain Erwin's mental health. So why did he decide to provide money? How did we come to be connected? What prompted his choice, exactly? How did he handle pressure? These were just some of the many inquiries he had to respond to.

Due to the possibility that a donor may have given up an organ for the wrong reasons, surgeons employ stringent interview procedures. They spoke of a farmer's wife who gave her husband a kidney but then filed for divorce as soon as she got out of the hospital. That was her mentality: "I've done my duty, now I can leave you for good." She had the idea that if she sold her kidney, she could get out of jail. I half-thought about whether or not people would see Erwin's live contribution as purely transactional. Even after all this time together, some people thought that Erwin just married me because of my wealth and not because he really loved me. With an older lady, what more could a younger guy want? Both Erwin and I knew it wasn't true, and he never seemed troubled by the rumours anyhow. They drove me insane while I was weak. Erwin has always been concerned just with me. After speaking with Erwin, the physicians confirmed my suspicions that he was not doing this for financial gain and that he was aware of the risks involved. Erwin was completely competent in his actions. Erwin's nature is such that he never has to second-guess his actions. His willingness to donate a kidney to me was the greatest gift imaginable—a gift of love.

Doctors finally agreed with me after years of observation: Erwin is in great physical form. In fact, he was so fit that his biological age was estimated to be lower than his chronological age (which, in my opinion, didn't make him younger than me since he still closed the blinds and locked the doors before going to bed, just like an old guy). With Erwin's kidney, I quipped, I'd be able to run the Boston Marathon in under three hours.

The physicians put us through a gruelling battery of exams. Erwin and I hit it off right away since we have the same blood type, A. However, this wasn't the only factor. Tissue typing was performed to determine how many antigens were shared between the donor and the recipient, and cross-matching was performed to foretell the recipient's reaction to the new kidney. If the cross match is positive, the recipient's immune system would reject the organ and there would be no way to do the transplant. We proved to be healthy enough to undergo the transplant procedure.

Erwin and I, meantime, had to watch our health. The only sound was that of the clock. I couldn't afford to lose even a fraction of my fortitude, vitality, or strength. Since I was not getting any younger, I naturally feared that there might be yet another delay or, God forbid, another difficulty. We were pleased to hear that things might finally progress. I was so prepared that I began keeping a calendar.

We drove the approximate two hours between Zurich and Basel to meet with the transplant group on many occasions. Basel is a prominent Swiss city and a river port on the Rhine, one of Europe's most important waterways. Even though I can't swim, I find water to be a fascinating sight. It's entirely visual that I like it so much. I like gazing out over Lake Zurich from my house because of the variety of colours it offers, the fact that it may move in any direction or stand completely still, and the possibility of seeing the sky in its reflection.

When we visited Basel, I felt the same feeling seeing the Rhine flow by. The river's flow through the city may be leisurely and placid on certain days, and swift and threatening on others. Cologne is a city in which the Rhine plays an integral role in daily life, so observing it always brought back fond memories of our time there. The time I spent with Erwin was a fresh beginning for me as an individual as well as a new beginning for us as a relationship. I always felt better after spending time along its banks. I saw several young folks lounging in the water and having a good time. The beauty that is life! I was hoping the Rhine would bring me a fresh start, as it has in the past.

Just as at the dialysis clinic in Zurich, Erwin meticulously scheduled our arrival to the hospital in Basel so that we could sneak in and exit without being seen. He drove into the garage below ground and led me by the hand to the entrance to the main building. About two hundred metres in length, the tunnel served as a physical barrier between the outside world and the inside world of the hospital. I saw parallels to Dante's River Styx, which separates the realms of the living and the dead. The whole time we were in there, I was on edge, and I kept an anxious eye out for signs that we were getting close to the door. There was no hidden entry, so we had to go through the Coca-Cola machine, the red walls that faded to grey and ultimately the lift that took us up to the hospital's main lobby. We were stealthy and hardly made a sound, and I often hid my face with a hood. We must have passed hundreds of individuals without nobody asking to take our picture. The Swiss are very unique!

Again, Professor Doctor Steiger took his time and made sure we understood every step of the transplant procedure. Again, I realised that I was the proverbial "cat with nine (or ten) lives." Tests revealed that my heart had been injured by so many years of high blood pressure; the muscle was enlarged and the veins were hardened, increasing the danger to which I was already exposed due to my recent malignancy. It was unclear whether or not a patient with a weak heart could handle the strain of surgery. The news was discouraging, but by this point I was accustomed to disappointments and wasn't about to let this one dampen my spirits.

Professor Doctor Steiger recognised my strength and determination. My heart passed his last evaluation, therefore we set the date for the transplant on April 7, 2017. The calmness and candour with which Erwin approached the impending operation impressed our physicians. Most donors experience significant anxiety, sometimes to the point where they are more terrified than the recipient. But not Erwin. He never lost his optimistic and steady demeanour. Not the same could be said of me. Because of the mental and physiological strain I had been under, my emotions were all over the place. Sometimes I'd become down on myself, and that would make me feel bad because I knew I ought to be thankful.

Setting up the two processes required much preparation. It takes two of everything: two operating rooms, two sets of surgical staff, and two patients to perform a successful organ transplant. The procedure on Erwin would go first.

Over the last five years, my family and I have focused our hopes and worries on my health problems. My husband Erwin was about to have a kidney removed from his body and transplanted into mine, and although I was reasonably nervous about the procedure, I was much more worried about him. As he described his "retroperitoneoscopic nephrectomy," I found myself unable to focus on what he was saying. After clipping the renal artery, the renal vein, and the ureter, the kidney may be taken from its protective fatty covering, rinsed with a cold special liquid, put on ice in a dish, and hurried to the recipient for transplantation.

When Erwin was being taken into the surgery room, I tried to block off any thoughts of these gruesome events. About an hour later, the surgeon gave the signal for the recipient to get prepared, and then it was my time. I was given medicine to relax me, and then I was transferred from my hospital bed to the operation table. There was a lot of light and motion in the space. People kept verifying with me that they had the proper patient for the appropriate procedure by asking me my name and the reason I was there. An electrode patch was placed on my chest, and a vein access device was affixed by a young guy. My eyes flickered and closed as the ventilator whirred and the anaesthesia began to work, and then I was unconscious.

The nurses were yelling my name and attempting to wake me the next thing I knew. Hours had passed, yet it seemed like I was still resting in the same position as when I'd closed my eyes. The operation was successful, I was informed, and all the physicians were relieved. Everything seemed surreal because I was so sleepy; the lights, noises, fragments of dialogue, and visits from the physicians and nurses. It took me a moment to realise that I had been transferred to the Intensive Care Unit, where I would begin my new life as a lady with a functioning kidney and a room full of what seemed like a hundred equipment. When I woke up the following day, I could think more clearly. After the procedure was over, I tentatively stretched my fingers and toes and found that I felt fine. The most amazing thing ever happened when the most stunning sight, wheelchair-bound Erwin, rolled into my room. When he came up to me and said, "Hi, darling!" he looked good—maybe even attractive. I felt such a range of emotions: joy, awe, and relief that we had survived.

Now that the operation was over, I was eager to hear the details. The physicians informed me that when I was lying on my back, Erwin was sprawled out on his side. The whole process took around two and a half hours, but the most important part—the transplant itself—took just a few minutes. It was fascinating to me that the normal procedure involves leaving ineffective organs like my kidneys. Three kidneys were now mine. As they detailed the momentous moment when my blood began to flow through Erwin's kidney, my new organ flared up brilliant red, showing signs of life, and I felt a shudder go up my spine. The effect was mystical.

We (Erwin and I) got well without a hitch. Erwin wheeled himself over to my bedside and conducted court, which brought a lot of joy and hilarity to the hospital where we were both patients. The team have experience caring for the elderly and ill. But Erwin, this young, vital guy who was donating a kidney to his older wife, was so charming that he was a pleasant distraction. My husband's collection of automotive periodicals, which he reads compulsively, delighted Professor Doctor Steiger. Erwin was obviously thinking forward to his next road trip.

My surgeon, Professor Doctor Gürke, was pleased with my progress. Since I was healthy and my physicians didn't expect any complications, I was released from the hospital after just seven days. Even quicker was Erwin's recuperation. Within a few of weeks, he was back to his old self and had his first drink of alcohol. Since then, he has not slowed down.

When I say "full speed ahead," I mean it. Six months after his operation, he and his biking buddies hit the open road across America. After that, we returned to the Basel medical centre for an examination, when Erwin complained of neck pain. The doctor said, "Yes, Mr. Bach." But that's not because of surgery or getting older; it's because of your Harley, man!

On the other side, my life has had its share of highs and lows. As is usual following a transplant, my body is fighting to reject the new kidney. In order to keep my antibodies from attacking a part of my body they don't recognise, I need to take very high dosages of immunosuppressants. Treatment might cause unpleasant side effects such as dizziness, amnesia, anxiety, and infrequent episodes of irrational diarrhoea, and can need further hospital stays. It's ironic because the reason I've never felt dizzy before is low blood pressure. I used to take up to twenty tablets a day, so I had to take them very methodically since I can't afford to make any errors.

In 2017, as December neared, I noticed an increase in my overall vitality. On November 26, we would be celebrating my birthday, and I was looking forward to having all of our closest friends over to our country home to do so. I usually appreciate the cards, messages, and even emails sent in celebration of my birthday, but this year's batch was especially touching after everything Erwin and I had through. I am not trying to push my luck; I fully expect my medical escapades to continue. Appointments, tests, and biopsies with doctors are constant after a transplant. However, I am still here, and so are you; in fact, we are closer now than we could have ever dreamed.

When I became giddy over getting new end tables for the living room, Erwin realised the old Tina (or maybe I was the new and better Tina) was back. Then I got out the Christmas decorations and made our house seem like a winter paradise. Decorating fever is a clear indication of life for me.

Finally, after years of illness, fear, desperation, and resignation, I was able to experience the pleasure of the holiday, the joy of life.

Tina was more familiar with rock 'n' roll than musical theater, so she made an effort to fill the knowledge gap by asking one of the manufacturers, Joop van den Ende, what the distinctions were between a fantastic rock concert and a musical. Tina started to see the parallels between the two creative forms when she discovered that a musical conveys a tale via songs. The concept of a musical adaption appealed to her more since she understood that her life was an amazing narrative in and of itself, with its own supporting melodies.

Tina eventually began to think that the musical would be a worthy project despite her initial skepticism. She had faith in the team, especially the Tennessee-born writer Katori Hall and a winner director Phyllida Lloyd, well known for their work on "Mamma Mia!" Tina Turner's initial trepidation, her struggle to comprehend the idea of a musical, and her final faith in the creative team driving the project were all characterized by her confidence that these great people would be able to do justice to her narrative and depict it accurately on stage. It demonstrates Tina's understanding of the significance of her own life narrative and the capacity of music to capture its essence. Tina Turner considers her role in the production of the musical based on her life, dubbed "Tina: The Tina Turner Opera." She states that she gave the project her approval and actively engaged in the process to make sure the narrative accurately reflected her experiences and feelings.

Turner admits that certain alterations and theatrical license are required when a memoir is made into a play. The most important thing to her was that the feelings conveyed were real, regardless of how the facts and events were changed. She wanted her life's experiences to be honestly portrayed in the musical, including both the good and the terrible, and to honor her close relationship to her music and audience.

Who would portray the part of Tina was a key issue for the musical. Adrienne Warren was selected for the part after a rigorous search. Turner praises Warren's ability and commitment, noting that she had to study Turner's songs, perfect her demeanor and choreography, and establish the persona while around the genuine Tina. Turner saw the difficulties Warren had in assuming such a legendary position and wanted to give her advice without making her uncomfortable.

Overall, Turner's engagement in the show was motivated by her drive to see her life story accurately portrayed and to encourage people via her rise from obscurity to fame throughout the world. She intended to communicate the strength of her pronunciation, her persistent optimism, and her will to live in spite of the challenges she encountered. who is probably Adrienne is receiving advise from Tina Turner on how to best represent her identity. The speaker makes it clear that being Tina entails more than just superficially copying her look with wigs, skirts, and heels. A deeper comprehension and connection are necessary.

The speaker notes that since Tina Turner's followers are so acquainted with her performances, they would evaluate and have high standards for anybody attempting to represent her. As a result, the speaker counsels Adrienne to put herself in Tina's position and not care about what other people say. Instead, she should concentrate on being genuine to herself.

The speaker provides Adrienne the chance to hear about his or her own experiences, feelings, and methods. Insights on phrasing, striking the proper notes, and perfecting recognizable routines like the hip shake and the Pony dance are all included in this. However, the speaker stresses how crucial it is to discover her own unique perspective and "inner Tina" in order to fully capture the spirit of the legendary singer.the difficulty of being Tina Turner, which necessitates a combination of taking inspiration from the original while also injecting one's own sincerity to properly become the persona. Tina Turner considers her post-transplant recuperation and future plans for retirement. At first, she thought she deserved the right to kick back, enjoy her improved health, and step down from public life. Erwin, her husband, had other plans for her, however. He wanted Tina to have an active role in the production of Tina: The Tina Turner The Musical, as well as the biography and documentary that would be made about her life.

Tina first opposed Erwin's ideas and wanted to unwind, but she eventually saw their advantages. She got countless cards and emails from people thanking her for sharing their stories, which caused her to rethink her plan to retire in silence. Tina saw her life's work as her legacy and felt driven to tell people about it. She also understood that there were issues from the past that needed to be expressed, and she wanted to say them in her own words.

Even though Tina yearned for a quiet recovery and retirement, she admits that collaborating on the musical and the book was beneficial to her while she was unwell. It offered her a feeling of direction, helped her stay focused, and gave her something to anticipate. Additionally, working on these projects gave her the chance to relive her memories, both good and bad, and acquire fresh perspective on her life.

Tina admits that, despite her early hesitation, Erwin's strategy to keep her occupied was successful in encouraging her to continue moving ahead, and she declares her love for him. She is aware that her longest relationship has been with her audience, and she is moved to return the favor by telling them her tale. After realizing the importance of her trip and the effect it has had on others, Tina is inspired to support Erwin's ideas and actively take part in the initiatives that will preserve her tale. Despite encountering tremendous obstacles, the author considers their own path towards attaining physical fitness and emotional well-being. The deadline for being in top condition for the announcement of a program starring Adrienne Warren on October 18, 2017, was that day. But given the writer's recent major transplant an operation, which was just six months old, this was a difficult assignment.

Due to the physical side effects of the procedure, the author shares their first worries and skepticism. They spoke about how corticosteroid prescription caused their face to swell, which also left them feeling cognitively clouded and had an impact on their memory. Their emotions were erratic, and their energy levels fluctuated. The risk of organ rejection further compelled the author to go often to Basel for examinations and medical checkups.

The author overcame all of these obstacles by gathering their courage and continuing. They mention that they wore a trim black Armani jacket, a vivid red shirt, and black slacks for the occasion. They took part in the opening rendition of the song "Proud Mary" next to Adrienne. The author shifted to the side and took a seat to observe while Adrienne sang on stage. The author couldn't help but exhibit their excitement and happiness by dancing and singing along in response to Adrienne's outstanding performance.the perseverance and resilience of the author in overcoming mental and emotional challenges to carry out their promises. Their successful involvement in the musical's opening and the enthusiastic response to Adrienne's performance left them with a feeling of achievement and hope for the future, despite their anxieties about performing in front of the media and fans. The legendary singer and actress Tina Turner recalls her time at the official premiere of the musical "Tina: The Tina Turner Musical," which is based on her life. She considers her feelings and actions during the performance as well as the importance of certain moments that were acted out on stage.

Tina chose a black Armani tuxedo for the evening, going for a timeless and subtle appearance. She was dressed elegantly in black Armani demi-gloves for a dramatic accent. Yet, Tina had met admirers on bicycles who accompanied her vehicle in an effort to collect a signature before she even reached the theater. She struggled because of her recent stroke, but she still succeeded in signing a few signatures before navigating the enthused masses.

Tina was pleasantly delighted when the crowd got up and cheered her when she first entered the theater. Since she was not the one singing on stage, she felt embarrassed and questioned why people were cheering for her. She quickly understood, however, that the event was a celebration of her life and an homage to her extraordinary journey. She was happy to see recognizable people in the crowd, such as Rod Stewart and John Knopfler, since the venue was packed to the gills.

Tina mentally and emotionally prepared herself for what she was going to see before the performance even started. Nam-myoho-renge-kyo, a well-known Buddhist chant, resounded around the auditorium to announce the beginning of the show. Her original song "Nutbush City Limits," which opened the event, received a fervent and passionate reception from the crowd.

Tina spotted characters from her own life, including her mother, grandmother, sister, children, and even her ex-husband Ike, throughout the whole production. Erwin, her present husband, sat next to her, ready to provide assistance and consolation as required.

Tina was deeply moved by the experience of having her life portrayed on stage as she watched the events take place. She understood the meaning of every phrase, but the performance seemed hurried due to the sets and songs changing so quickly. Her favorite moments, however, were when "River Deep—Mountain High" was performed.

For Tina, this song was very important since it marked a turning point in her life. Working on this song with Phil Spector gave her new insight about singing and life. It symbolized her coming to terms with her independence, sense of worth, and desire for more out of life. Tina and the audience were both moved by this part in the musical, underscoring its impact and significance on her path.

The dramatization of the domestic abuse Tina experienced while dating Ike was one of the musical's most anticipated elements, according to both Tina and the audience. She acknowledges that remembering her background still makes her feel strong emotions and may sometimes cause nightmares. Her life and the abuse she endured are depicted in the film "What is Love Got to Do with It," which she has decided not to view. As she describes her responses to the musical and considers the crucial times in her life, Tina Turner's sensitivity and tenacity come through. She recognizes the influence of her experiences, both good and bad, and how they have helped to make her the strong and motivational person she is today. the narrator considers their own history as well as the psychological trip they have taken in light of their past. They add that because of their unresolved sentiments against Ike Turner, their ex-partner, they had never seen the movie "What is Love Got to Do about It." They do, however, think about whether it would be simpler for them to see the musical version of their life story.

While undergoing treatment in a hospital in Switzerland, the narrator had a profound moment of reflection as they struggled with uncertainties over their well-being as well as their They remember, though, reclining comfortably in the greatest seat in the house during the musical's debut in London from a different viewpoint. They claim to be in a different place today, physically as well as mentally, which implies personal development and healing.

When they see the musical, they say it is like witnessing their own tale while realizing it is not their own. They stress that nothing bad can happen to them now, despite what is presented on stage. Unexpectedly, instead of sobbing as they would have anticipated, they start laughing instead, not because it is humorous but rather because of how bizarre and uncanny it is to see their history play out in front of them.

Kobna Holdbrook-Smith, who plays Ike, especially impresses the narrator since he flawlessly captures Ike's look, voice, and mannerisms. The narrator responds in an unexpected way in response to this eerie likeness. They admit to accepting their history and find comfort in sometimes being able to joke about it. Recognizing the skill, vigor, and passion of the musical's cast and crew, they take satisfaction in knowing that their legacy is in good hands. a pivotal scene in which the musical's rendition of "Proud Mary" causes the audience to react passionately. The narrator experiences a time travel to a joyful, animated setting reminiscent of a sacred chapel. The audience's rousing applause as well as their overwhelming affection and kindness move the storyteller to tears. They take advantage of the chance to address the audience, expressing their adoration for Adrienne, the actress who is playing them, and announcing that they may finally retire now that they have found a deserving successor.As the narrator watches their own life narrative play out on stage, they go on a journey of self-reflection, acceptance, and closure. They emphasize the musical's ability to change them and the therapeutic impact it has had on them. They also express their thanks to the audience for their love and support. The speaker considers their life path, which is represented by their change from Anna Mae to the well-known singer Tina Turner. They discuss looking at Kobna Holdbrook-Smith, who is probably an actress portraying their ex violent spouse Ike Turner. Even if the speaker has unpleasant recollections of Ike, the fact that he has forgiven him shows that he has grown and healed.

The speaker then considers the difficulties they have encountered in life, such as a tumultuous upbringing, an unhappy marriage, and numerous hindrances depending on their gender, age, and race. They have persisted and moved forward in spite of these obstacles. They talk about their present boyfriend, Erwin, and how happy they are with him, but they also emphasize the time when they were on the verge of losing everything and how love saved them.

the speaker considers their life's path and the difficulties they have faced. The speaker admits the lack of affection in their early life as they reflect on their modest beginnings as a youngster in Nutbush. They persevered and went forward in spite of this.

The speaker describes their difficult marriage and how it almost ended their relationship. They had to overcome a number of challenges, including prejudice determined by their sexual orientation, age, and race, but they refused to allow these defeats define them. Instead, they decided to keep going.

The speaker then says that they found happiness with a man called Erwin, but she also says that they nearly lost everything. But love finally delivered them from this situation. The speaker highlights that they are still moving ahead in life despite the difficulties they have encountered. The speaker's closing remarks to the listeners and readers reflect their outlook on life. They use an ancient Buddhist adage when they claim that it is possible to transform poison into medicine. This idiom captures the speaker's conviction that adversity and difficulty may be turned into chances for development and progress. resilience, tenacity, and optimism of the speaker in the face of difficulty. Although they are aware of the challenges they have faced, they choose to concentrate on the benefits and the ability to change their own life story. It conveys the concept that even in the most trying situations, one may discover significance and power.

The speaker's last remarks to the listeners, and afterwards to the reader, capture their general philosophy of life. They take their cue from an ancient Buddhist adage that asserts that whatever unpleasant or destructive may be changed into something constructive. This statement expresses the speaker's fortitude and capacity to triumph over challenges, implying that they have used their previous suffering as a source of ability and expertise. It spreads a message of empowerment and optimism, empowering people to develop their own inner strength and conquer their own obstacles.

Who would portray the part of Tina was a key issue for the musical. Adrienne Warren was selected for the part after a rigorous search. Turner praises Warren's ability and commitment, noting that she had to study Turner's songs, perfect her demeanor and choreography, and establish the persona while around the genuine Tina. Turner saw the difficulties Warren had in assuming such a legendary position and wanted to give her advice without making her uncomfortable.

Overall, Turner's engagement in the show was motivated by her drive to see her life story accurately portrayed and to encourage people via her rise from obscurity to fame throughout the world. She intended to communicate the strength of her pronunciation, her persistent optimism, and her will to live in spite of the challenges she encountered.

Printed in Great Britain
by Amazon

bee26593-9c83-4050-87f4-511d1a48c40dR01